ILLEGAL CITIZENS

SALAAM PRESS PUBLICATION

Published in the United States of America by
Salaam Press, LLC
info@salaampress.com
www.salaampress.com

Front cover design by Leila Hosseini
Front cover photography by by Hemali Acharya

Leila Hosseini contact information:
e-mail: leila.hosseini@salaampress.com
website: http://www.salaampress.com

Hemali Acharya contact information:
e-mail: hemali@hemaliphotography.com
website: http://www.hemaliphotography.com

ISBN 0-9800138-8-7 978-0-9800138-8-7

ALSO BY AFDHERE JAMA

At Noonday with the Gods of Somalia

ILLEGAL CITIZENS

queer lives in the muslim world

AFDHERE JAMA

NOTICE ABOUT IMAGES AND NAMES

The names of the people in this book have been changed in order to respect and protect their privacy. Likewise, the images that appear in the book are solely there to connect these lives with the places they call home. None of the people in the images have any connections with the subjects that are featured.

for everyone whose love is illegalized.

CONTENTS

ACKNOWLEDGEMENTS

The first story I ever wrote was about Hamdi, a Somali transsexual whom I met in Seattle. I was fascinated by her journey, and the courage she undertook to live the simple life she envisioned for herself: to live like the woman she always knew she was. Five years later, I revisited her for *The Gabdho of Somalia*, which chronicles her story from running away home to finding a community in a city far away, to coming America. I knew how much she risked because I, too, a queer Somali, experienced some of the pains of growing up in a culture where you have no place whatsoever. I remember being overwhelmed by feelings of gratitude and respect for her. I thought it was amazing how this woman told me everything that was dear about her life.

Thirty-three stories later, from twenty-two of countries, I still feel the same gratitude for the people that lived them.

I want to take a moment and say thank you. Words simply cannot convey how grateful I'm for everything your lives have brought to mine. I'm a better person today because of the personal connection I have with everything you experienced—good, bad, and ugly.

There are also many people behind the book. Someone, somewhere, somehow introduced me or led me to each individual whose life I have followed. There are those I wish to thank by name, including because they really went out of their way:

Allison A., Naser Abdulhakeem, Rehman Aboudi, Tarek Ahmed, Rachida Ali, James Baker, Jamila Bilal, Farha Baroudi, Duran F., Shahid Fiaz, Burcu G., Cem Görgün, Malek H., Suha Habbash, Ayman Hassan, Leila Hosseini, Hadiyo Jim'ale, Sa'ido Kahin, Bassam Kassab, Nilofer Khan, Nabila M., Faisal Nouradine, Jameelah Nouri, Mehmet O., Dede Oetomo, JS Omar, Faiza Omerovic, Mohamed Riyale, Mahdi Tariq, Özlem Z., and Ali Zulfe.

And some of these people even traveled with me, translated for me, and helped me understand the very cultures I wrote about. I can't thank you enough.

I thank you for your patience, love, and support. But, most of all, I thank you for your dedication to tell our stories!

Although people have told me their stories, and there were those who got me to them, this book is what it is today because of many more. I want to thank the people who supported me throughout the process of getting this book out:

I thank Sharifa Ismail for the love, emotional support, and for financing some of the projects herself although she is an Iraqi woman and even if sometimes the subjects were men in countries she has never been. Thank you very much!

I want to thank Jennifer Ahmed, who was always my lifeline and slept with her cellphone under her pillow just in case something happened to me while in the mountains of Afghanistan or the jungles of Indonesia or wherever else I happened to be at that moment. I know all the things you have done for me, Jennifer, and I sincerely thank you—I will never be able to repay you!

Abu Omar, my dear friend and colleague, who never let me forget why I was doing what I was doing whenever I would get discouraged by all the horrible things that happen in the world; he supported me always professionally as well by single-handedly taking over *Huriyah* whenever I needed him to. I would be lost without you. Thank you for everything.

Leila Hosseini—my Persian superwoman whom I had the pleasure of enjoying her very much human abilities of unconditional love, dedication and support. They say people come into your life for a reason. I love you very much, and thank you for EVERYTHING!

Also, Daayiee Abdullah—for your friendship, encouragement and counsel. Thank you!

My mother, who passed away during the gathering of the book. You helped me so much when you were alive in understanding that love is all that matters in the world. It is with that love I celebrate the lives of those I encounter, and I thank you for that. I love you, mama.

THIS IS WHY...

About five years ago, as this book was coming together, a correspondent for *Huriyah* in Morocco asked me, "Why are you publishing a book about queer Muslims?" To say this question took me by surprise would be the understatement of the century. I was shocked. It was shocking to me mainly because it came from a woman with whom I thought I shared a common interest in what I thought was the bettering visibility of the lesbian, gay, bisexual, transgender, transsexual, or otherwise queer Muslim community.

Like millions of queer Muslims out there, unfortunately, my friend had been conditioned to believe that our stories don't matter as much as everyone else's stories of love, hate, and everything in between—what makes us human. I remember being a teenager and asking an older cousin of mine if there are homosexual Muslims after we saw something on television about Christian gays coming out. He said, "We don't have those kind of people in Islam."

And, like so many queer Muslims, my friend lives in a country where she is an illegal citizen—whose love and sexuality is not only unrecognized but also punished. In some Muslim countries, there are even active groups in law enforcement whose job pertains to nothing else but eliminating homosexuals in their societies.

This is exactly why I wanted to document the lives of the queer Muslims in this book. It is the same reason why I wanted to start a queer Muslim magazine, or why I decided to make films about issues relating to sexuality, faith, race, and other interests of my communities. If I don't, I asked myself at every stage, then who will? We are millions worldwide. But we are powerless because we are voiceless. We are muted into submission.

And not just by Islamists.

For many years, I had been reading gay and lesbian magazines here in the safe West that did not talk about queer Muslim issues. Cover after cover, a magazine after a magazine, I was silently told, "You don't exist." Never, ever have I seen a queer Muslim that wasn't objectified on level or another on any nationwide gay or lesbian newspaper or magazine. So I started one and called it "freedom"—freedom from them all; the islamists, the islamophobes, and the homophobes on all sides of the world. Many years later, *Huriyah* is now reaching cities whose names I can't even pronounce. I get letters everyday that people are changed—over seventy countries and counting. And best of all, we keep it free of charge!

I had been reading books on queer issues in the Muslim community written by non-Muslims or by straight Muslims—neither who could really relate to the issues from within. When we read books by the traditional Muslim community, which views us through heterosexual normative, we are sinners if we act upon our natural sexual desires.

I watched films that saw us through the lens of the Western eye. I have seen films by Muslims hijacked by irrational understanding of sexuality, desire and love.

But when there was an article in a gay and lesbian publication, or there was a film or a book on these issues, they often lacked the ability to show the diversity of the community.

Diversity is precisely why I wanted to focus on the world rather than a particular country. I was shocked by the sheer diversity of the Muslim World. For example, I remember going to a party in one of Tehran's conservative neighborhoods. I was conditioned to fear Iran, and I was waiting for the door to be broken down by the Secret Police all night—leading to my being arrested in a country I was in illegally, where I could be hanged and no one would have known. As fully explored in the story entitled *The Tehranian*, Hossein, the man who took me to the party, is a gay man who lives a complicated life that defies all stereotypes. By day, he is the conservative son of a powerful ayatollah. By night, he risks everything by being true to himself in one of the world's most dangerous countries for gay people by doing basic human things like meet other gay friends, or go to a dance party, or even spend the night with his boyfriend.

Would Hossein's story be covered in many of the American magazines? Would it be featured on any television show? Would someone write about it in a book? No. His bravery is of no interest to those who want to paint a Muslim as either a terrorist, hell-bent on destroying the world, or a poor victim of a backward religion, or as the sad and the permanent victims of a post-9/11 American Islamophobia. Not because many of these educated people who ran the media actually believe this crap but because they know very well that is what sells in these times.

But, Hossein and millions of others are living interesting lives if people wanted to know.

Speaking of Hossein, he once traveled with me to Mashhad, where a young gay couple was hanged, and I was so angry at the time because it was just too horrible as they were so young that I was not seeing those living around me. He had already introduced me to many young gay and lesbian Iranians who were living their lives, and most of whom I considered brave because I wasn't sure I would be able to do the things they were willing to do in a country like theirs.

Anyway, one night after we left a safe house where I had just met a relative of one the kids hanged, and I freely expressed my deep shame to be a Muslim in a country like Iran where family can allow your name to be forgotten simply because you are homosexual, Hossein stood in the middle of the street and said to me, "I'm alive. There are millions of gays alive in this country. We want to be heard. Why don't you tell our stories?"

I felt paralyzed.

He was so right. I knew Hossein for many years, and it never occurred to me to tell his story. This was precisely because, like my Moroccan friend, I was conditioned. I realized then that I had a long way to go in battling these demons out of my system.

Of course, by telling the story of the living does not mean we forget those whose lives are wrongfully taken. The case of Ayaz and Mahmoud, who were murdered in a broad daylight simply because they were gay, had already been so widely covered. At one point, the story was everywhere that my own life was in danger in Saudi Arabia, where I had been following another story, because idiotic journalists were trying to track me down everywhere. I mean, really, how many Somali guys are running around in small town Saudi Arabia, trying to figure out a mess?

Saudi Arabia, by the way, is another example of a country where brave people live. While I was researching about the story of Amr, a young man murdered by his family and whose story I detailed in *Somewhere in Hijaz*, I was shocked how gay life in Saudi Arabia was so far from everything I ever thought about. One day, as I sat in a coffee shop thinking about what happened to that poor guy, I found myself being cruised by a beautiful man. He was probably in his thirties, and was clearly gay—he wore a bright pink shirt, under his white *khameez*. Later, he took me to a party in Jeddah, attended by flamboyant boys and drag queens. I was shocked at how at ease they were about the whole thing. They worried none. I, a foreigner, was far more worried about their safety. I remember thinking, "This is Saudi Arabia! This is Saudi Arabia!"

But the most interesting thing happened later. On my way back from 'Umrah, my friend Abu Omar, who by the way happens to be a Saudi living in Cairo, called me.

"Are you still in the Holy Land?"

He was my main contact, and was keeping an eye out for me, so I freaked out thinking the Saudi authorities were onto me. He said, so casually. "There is a wedding in Medina. I just thought that maybe you would you like to go?"

My response was immediate: "Are you crazy? No! I'm too tired. I want to sleep for days!"

It turned out the wedding was a gay one—between a Saudi man and his longtime Indonesian partner. I thought if there is a gay wedding in the second holiest city in the Muslim World today, I really don't have to tell anyone's story.

We have come along way. But as you read this book, I'm sure you will realize that there is much to be done. Those of us who live in safe countries in the West, we often forget that the rights we so enjoy today did not come overnight; that men and women fought for these rights. I recently saw a documentary called *Screaming Queens* on how transsexuals in San Francisco literally went into the streets with "Enough!"—bitch-slapping the local police, long before the Stonewall riots in New York. But it wasn't violence that got the attention of the mainstream West. It was people telling the stories of everyday people, and humanizing our faces—allowing for room those others to see us outside their televised news objectifications of gays and lesbians.

As queer Muslims, I think, we can learn a lot from the history of the queer West. Think about this—what can you do in your country today? For some, it means joining a local queer organization. In countries like Nigeria, Lebanon, Turkey, Bosnia, et cetera, this is possible. For others, it means merely helping in more underground ways such as helping those who cannot live in their homes as is the case in Iran, for example, where there are countless underground groups who are actively helping people resettle in different parts of the country.

There are many ways to help. But, please, I beg you, consider helping.

love in lagos

Nigeria. Just the name of it brings up so much. In Africa when we think of this beautiful country, it is always the population that first comes to mind. It is the most populated country in the continent with an estimated hundred-and-forty million people, which also ranks it ninth in the world. But population is not the only wonder. Nigeria has the largest African cinema, often called *Nellywood*—popular as far as Japan and Australia. The country is also one of the oil-rich soils in the world.

Here, the rivers Niger and Benue come together... hold hands... and follow each other into the Gulf of Guinea. Not far from there lies a city called Lagos. It is the former capital, with nothing 'former' and everything current. It remains to be the largest city in the country, with more than fifteen million people. It is most certainly one of the fastest growing cities in the world, and the largest in Black Africa.

Bolaji was born here, to a Muslim family of Yoruba-Hausa background. His great grandfather came to Lagos in the early 1900s as a young man to work in the city, which was then beginning to become a success. He was Hausa and hailed from the north. Once in Lagos, the man fell deeply in love with a Yoruba Christian woman. Without his family's knowledge or approval, he married her. By the time they found out, she was already a Muslim.

Bolaji's story is somewhat similar, with a bit more heartache.

"When I was little, my neighbor boy and I used to play with each other," says Bolaji, with a smile. "It was innocent. Nothing mischievous. Then once in secondary school, everything become mischievous, of course," he adds, with a chuckle.

That boy is Yarow. Yarow is actually not even Nigerian. When Bolaji was five, seven year-old Yarow's family moved to Lagos from Kampala, Uganda. A prominent Christian family, they fled the oppression of Idi Amin and sought refuge in Nigeria. "I feel lucky that his family chose to live next to us," says Bolaji.

Whatever childhood fun they have had, the young men thought perhaps it would dangerous to continue doing what they were doing. "Then I told him that I loved him," says Bolaji. "He did not like it and ran off. I hadn't seen him for months. Then, one day he turned up. He said he could not get away from the feelings. He was in love with me, too. I was so happy."

Everything was good.

"Then came the 'Now what?' of course," says Bolaji, "we were both from wealthy families. Our culture is horribly homophobic. People in this country hate you for no reason. Any expression of love between two people of the same sex is considered horrendous. We did not want anyone to suffer because of us."

They tried to live secretly, quietly without any giving any hints. Bolaji says that did not work at all. The men were so in love that it had become clear to everyone who spent a minute with them.

"I come from a very business-minded family," says Bolaji, a 32-year-old architect, "from both sides, but especially in my father's side. We are a business people, and business peoples have no time for religion. We are culturally both Muslim and Nigerian. We go to the *masjid* [mosque] but as a cultural meeting place, and we also go to our spirit dances. But Yarow comes from a devoutly Christian family. We knew exactly how they would feel about homosexual love."

The couple went to Bolaji's mom. She did not deal with the news as well as they thought. She became very angry, turning extremely manipulative by telling the guys they could either leave town or she would expose them to the rest of the family. When they tried to use the "we have no money" trick, she provided money—and lots of it.

Afraid of what might happen if they stayed, the men decided to leave. "We had no choice," says Bolaji, "we had to go. Yarow's family was very well connected in Lagos. We both remembered how they sent one of their own sons to prison for charges of corruption at the church he was maintaining. Who knows what they would do to us?"

Not wanting to find out, the men decided to go to Port Harcourt. Another city by the waters, Port Harcourt was not a familiar town to either of the men. All they knew was a common friend from their high school days. And unlike Lagos, this new city proved to be a bit hostile to the men.

"The first day we arrived, we lost two bags," says Bolaji, laughing. "And I got punched in the face when I laughed at a man making a funny face. And Yarow lost—well, it was stolen—his Rolex watch. On our way to the hotel, my hat flew away. Just not good way to start out in a new city."

Within a week, they were back in Lagos.

Outraged by their return, Bolaji's mother vowed to tell his father after the Ramadan, which was two months away, had passed. This gave the couple time to prepare for the worst. "We were ready," says Bolaji. "We didn't care anymore. This was our home city. We were not going anywhere else. If mother wanted to out us, we would deal with that."

When that Ramadan had passed, the mother decided not to expose the men. Instead, she begged and pleaded for her son to stop being gay. After a while, Bolaji says the mother had come around when she realized she was unsuccessful. While she does not accept the relationship, she stopped taunting Bolaji about it. She had also agreed to keep their secret from the father, who is battling diabetes and high blood pressure, until his health improves. Bolaji thinks everyone else knows but pretends they don't know.

In the meantime, the couple moved in together in one of the suburbs—Ikeje, a somewhat quiet district. Bolaji now owns his own film business in Surulere, a district that never sleeps, while Yarow, like many in this city, works in the business district of the Lagos Island. They go about their day, frustrated with traffic like most Lagonians. At night, they come home to each other.

"It is a cruel, repetitive life," jokes Bolaji, sharing a laugh with Yarow, "I love this man but he won't let us be more adventurous. I would rather we travel the world and worry about where we will find an eatery next. Do you not think it would be nice to get lost in Australia or South America? But now we have a typical, predictable life. Maybe one day I will convince him to live out more!"

In a country with a majority of violently homophobic people, Bolaji says he wishes things were different. "It would be nice to be able to show affection in public and not get persecuted for it," he says, "within our circles of friends and colleagues it is okay. This society is not ready. Everything is against us here."

For now, living in love—however quietly—seems to be plenty.

the gabdho of somalia

"Oh, it is beautiful being a *gabadh* [girl]," says Hamdi, a Somali transsexual who now lives in Bellingham, Washington. "Somali men treat you better. I really enjoy my days as a woman better than when I was a guy."

Hamdi, who has gone through a gender reassignment surgery, was born a male child. The proud parents named the boy Sa'id. Later, she named herself Hamdi, an Arabic name that translates "to be thankful," when she moved to a new community that was more accepting.

"The name goes with how I felt. I was thankful to be who I was. It just came to me one night and in the morning, I told everyone I wanted to be called that name."

As a boy, Hamdi says she thought she was gay but also knew there was something different about the way she felt about guys. "I wasn't just another guy," she says. "I was a girl inside a guy's body. This was very confusing to a teen who did not even know there was such thing as a transsexual."

She even once told a guy, after she fell in love with him how she felt she was a woman inside.

"He freaked out. I remember he was shaking and was trying not to touch me. He was gay and I just told him I was a woman, how would anyone feel? It was a shock."

Hamdi, who originated from the northern Somali state of Waqooyi, ran away after that incident to the southern capital Mogadishu. "I packed my bags and boarded on a bus the next morning," she recalls. "Next stop, Hamar [Mogadishu]. That was one of the wildest things I have ever done. I was scared. Fear makes you do all sorts of strange things."

There she found communities in which, she was told, she could live as gay or as anything else she wanted to be and would be accepted. "It was like a dream come true for me," says the now 29-year-old woman, who became a nurse after she had moved to the U.S. six years ago. "I immediately moved to

Hamar-Jajab [a district in Mogadishu.] It wasn't easy having to find a place to live and work, but it was the best thing that I have ever done for myself."

Hamdi says she found the community there exactly what she was looking for; gay men wearing women's clothing. "I thought 'this is it.'"

A whole village of gay men dressed as women became a bit too much later, however, recalls the well dressed tall woman.

"Suddenly, the reality hit," she says, polishing her nails as she sighs. "I was confronted with an entire district that was like me. Even though it was very nice to be accepted, I realized I was one of the lucky ones there. Not everything seemed as rosy."

Soon, she found out that those gay men who did not want to dress as women were not welcome. In fact, she says, "they were chased away from the neighborhood whenever they came around there to pick up drag queens. It was horrible. I was not attracted to drag queens, I was attracted to men who dressed like other men," she recounts. "But I was not allowed to be with them. No, you had to punish them and chase them away. It was very strange."

Because she was young and broke, Hamdi was smart enough to realize she had to put up with whatever rules she was told to follow. But she met straight men on the side and was able to carry out love affairs with the kinds of men she wanted.

"I had to sneak around," she remembers, "but I definitely broke all the rules."

After the civil war broke out in Somalia, Hamdi finally got the freedom she desired. She went to a Kenyan refugee camp outside of Mombasa. Once there, she met others who were in the same situation as her.

"After a few years of making life there, I was able to emigrate to the United States," says Hamdi.

Today, she has no desire for her old roots. She fears for her safety and does not wish to go back to her country.

"I think I became too American," she says, fondling her red hair. "It would be foolishness to think I can just go back and everything will be like old times. Everything has changed. The Somali community has changed, and so have I."

A few years after she immigrated to America, Hamdi met a Somali man. The couple met in college, and developed a friendship. Without knowing about her gender history, the man fell in love with a woman he called a fighter.

"For the first time in my life, I met someone who loved me completely," she says of the man. "I didn't have the heart to tell him everything. I was scared of losing him. After all, he was a Somali man and God knows about my people and their ideas."

So for years she hid her past. He started to bug her about marriage, which she was not ready for until she told him her secret. A few years ago, she could no longer keep it up. She told him everything.

"He disappeared for nearly a month," she remembers.

Since then, he came back and the two continued their lives—even getting married. Today, a quiet life replaces her traumatic past.

"Life is too short," says Hamdi, "and marriage has been a long dream for me. And I'm very grateful that it has finally come true."

dreaming in swahili

It is no wonder at all that Stone Town became the most populated area of the island of Zanzibar. Because it is right in the middle of the island, but on the west coast, it was a stop over between the Spice Islands—Zanzibar, Pemba and Mafia. Zanzibar is the largest island of the three. Over the centuries, the town has grown very diverse. Walking along the stone houses in the villages, you will run into people of all sorts of racial backgrounds—Arab, Indian, Bantu and even Chinese.

Here, women are perhaps the most important part of society. They are the hardest working citizens. Everything relies on women. Because it is deeply believed life is nothing without family, marriage is hence considered a top priority for a woman. So when Roha—a young Muslim woman from a tiny village outside of the town—refused marriage, her family was understandably upset. The Muslims, who are the majority of the Island, have a tradition of marrying off their daughters young.

"My mother was the hardest on me," recalls Roha, whose name means "soul" in Swahili. "She told me I had to get married. What would I do with my life without marriage? My answer was very clear: I wanted to work for me, not for a husband and children. My mother did not understand this desire to be independent, and have ta ken it as offense to the culture and even to herself."

Everyone said she would get over it, but Roha continued to be single—turning down every marriage proposal that came her way. Her village, which is almost all Muslim, was so worked up over her refusal that one of the rejected men even tried to rape her so he would be forced to marry her. This happened when she was twenty-three. Instead of succumbing to societal pressure to get married, Roha moved out of Zanzibar and into Dar es Salaam, the capital of Tanzania.

"Dar is bigger," says Roha, "I can hide here without a problem. No one worries about me not being married. In fact, most people don't even care.

Everyone is so busy with his or her life. They have no time to have concerns for a Zanzibari girl."

Islam in Tanzania is growing more and more towards a strict interpretation as other countries in East Africa like Somalia, Ethiopia and Kenya. And this has forced women like Roha to find solace in communities outside. However, after she moved out to Dar es Salaam, Roha befriended an imam whom she says has saved her drained Muslim soul.

"He just spoke to me in terms I could find comfort," she says of the Arusha-born Ismaili scholar of Indian background. "At first, he was trying to discourage me away from lesbianism but once he realized that I really was a lesbian he became softer. He said there are enough women who are straight to carry the world and that Allah loves me the way I am. That no matter what I do, I should never give up on Allah's mercy, which he told me is beyond what anyone can lay out. Since then, I became less and less judgmental and more loving towards myself."

Although she has not completely reconciled her faith with her sexuality, Roha says she can tell her life has changed. Going to Mosque for Friday prayers are no longer something she feels torn about. The 32-year-old is now finally coming into herself, learning what works for her and what doesn't. And still unmarried, she makes her living working as a maid for a rich Somali family in the city.

"They are Muslim," she says, "so it is easier to work for them unlike my last employer, who happened to have no faith and morals. He was successful single man and tried to violate me several times. I can take care of myself, but it helps if I don't have to fight so much. With this family, things are less chaotic although I wonder if they would be had they knew about my sexuality."

A few years earlier, Roha recalls working for a large Italian family. The husband—who was twice Roha's age—hit on her so much that she quit the job.

"Not because he was not attractive," says Roha, "but because I'm a lesbian. I fancy other women, not men—and especially not married men. So when it became obvious that he was not letting me do my work peacefully, I just left them."

In Zanzibar, and most of Tanzania, there is no place in society for lesbians, says Roha. This is why when she returns home every three months, she tries her "best to be as feminine as" she can, she says.

She gets dirty stares. As if she has a disease, people avoid touching her. People talk about her behind her back. They spread rumors about her. It hurts her, Roha says, but she understands. She is not as feminine as a woman should be according to her culture. And femininity is something she lost, she says, after she left home.

"Here I'm like a man," Roha says, almost complaining. "I go to work every morning, and I come here at night. But my house is empty, so I used to go out with other *wasagaji* [lesbians]. That is our lives. We have no choice. There is no family to hold us down. Sometimes this is good for us, and other times it is not something we want."

Overall, Roha is happy to be on her own even if it means she gets less sleep and lives in an empty room in a bad neighborhood. There are prizes to be claimed.

"Right now, I have big dreams," she says, "I have high hopes for my future. So I will endure anything."

Working as a maid through the years, Roha put herself in sewing school. She now sews most of her free time. "I make *kitenge* and other African clothing," she says, "and then my friend who runs a store in the market sells them to the tourists."

It is not much but she makes some income from it, which, combined with her maid salary, she hopes to buy a home someday.

"My biggest dream is to own a house facing the sea in Bagamoyo [small town north of Dar es Salaam]. It is going to cost me a lot of money but I'm working on it!"

Why would she leave the life of the city for a small town?

"Because I want to have a wife there," she says, laughing out loud as if she is hearing herself for the first time, "it is my dream. Big house, big woman and the sea."

In the meantime, she is single. And living in the city, big women are all around.

hot nights in darfur

El-Fashir is the capital of Sham el Darfur or North Darfur, a region in the largest country in Africa—Sudan. It was found by a tribe called Fur; hence the name Darfur, which in Arabic means "the home of the Fur people." The region was an independent Sultanate for hundreds of years before the conquest of Egypt in the late 1800s. Later in the early 1900s, the British annexed it to Sudan.

Since 2003, Darfur has been the battleground between the Janjaweed, armed militia group from varies Black people who consider themselves Arabs, and other Blacks such as the Fur people, as well as the Zaghawa and Massaleit.

In a camp outside of El Fashir, a 34-year-old gay man named Omar works with an aid group. His belongs to the Fur tribe. At the time of this writing, the Janjaweed have already attacked this very camp more than a dozen times this year alone. And it is only September. Everyday, he risks death. But he is not a Fur here.

"I work here under the citizenship of a foreign country I would rather not mention," says Omar. "I don't want to be part of this conflict, I want to be part of the solution."

In a small village west of Darfur, near the Chad border, rebels from his tribe recruited Omar to join the Harakkat tahrir el Sudan also known as the Sudan Liberation Army (SLA). He spent months training, and was a nomad moving from village to another in hopes of librating his people from the Janjaweed.

"It was a hard life," Omar remembers, "but I wanted to be part of it. I thought I was defending my people, and that it was the best thing for Sudan in general. Of course, there is nothing good about war or being a soldier. It is just what you say to yourself in order to go on, or in order to be able to kill another human being."

For Omar, the stakes got higher when a Janjaweed group captured him. One day, as he was trying to get water from a *wadi* or a riverbank, he felt a gun rest against the back of his heart. The man commanded not to make any moves, says Omar.

"I turned around," he remembers, " and he hit me with the gun so hard I felt dizzy. But he didn't let me fall. I'm sure this does not make sense to anyone but there was a tender feeling in that. I felt it as soon as he motioned. He didn't want me to fall."

It turned out that the man was just giving a show but that he actually did not want to harm Omar. He and his friends took Omar back to a village controlled by the Janjaweed. Omar was to be held as a prisoner of war because they couldn't decide whether he was useful to them or not. The man who hit him earlier, named Ahmed, was given the task of guarding Omar.

"As soon as we were alone, he apologized," says Omar, smiling. "I told him I understood why he did what he did, and that I appreciated his care that he did not let me fall. Although I had no idea he might be attracted to me, I expressed the truth and said I was madly attracted to him. To my surprise, he leaned over and kissed me. He kissed me on the lips. I almost fainted. I really did not expect this. I thought that even if he was attracted to me, which I doubted very much, he would restrain himself."

That night, the two had sex very quietly.

Later, after the last man slept, Ahmed told Omar that he would take him to his village or another village controlled by the SLA. Omar was not sure if this was a good idea. What if they were caught? The Janjaweed would kill them both. But Ahmed insisted to take the risk because he knew Omar had a bigger risk if he stayed prisoner. If the Janjaweed thought he was not useful, they would not think twice about killing him.

"We had to be very quiet," says Omar. "We rode his horse until we were about a mile away from my village. Then we had to say goodbye. I wanted us to run away together. To Chad, where I knew people. But Ahmed was not in a position to leave. His wife was having a child in matter of days. He wanted to see his child. Ahmed kept saying that we would meet again after there is peace, but I was not as optimistic."

Ahmed rode back to his men to face the consequence.

"The Janjaweed are scornful," says Omar. "They don't forgive betrayal. And certainly this would be a clear betrayal against his commander. I would be surprised if he was not punished severely."

Omar went on to his village that night, almost getting killed because they thought he was an enemy. Why would anyone be walking that late? Alone? In times of war? He could have been a Janjaweed—a spy.

But that night changed Omar's life.

"I realized I could no longer go to war against the Janjaweed," he says. "I could not with good conscious go to war knowing Ahmed is on the other side and I could kill him, or he could kill me. I tried to imagine what my life would be like if I had known I killed him. It was easy to let go because the hatred I had for the Janjaweed was replaced by my love for Ahmed. I wanted to be part of the peace. I wanted to see him alive again."

But it is not easy to leave the SLA or any other rebel group. It would be seen as a betrayal against one's people. Like all of the men in the rebel groups, Omar made a living elsewhere. He was a merchant who brought goods between Darfur and Chad.

"These are men from villages," says Omar, "they have wives and children and family in these villages. No one supports them abroad so they must make a living somehow. Thank God we live in a country with so many resources. I chose to be a merchant because I get along with people well."

In his next trip to Chad, he just never came back. He left Chad, went to another country, gotten himself a fake citizenship, went to Khartoum as a foreigner and joined an aid group. It is a long way to come back to the same country, but Omar says it was worth it.

"No one knows me in El Fashir," he says, confidently, "I can live here without any trouble. I can wait my Ahmed here. Some days, I think he will walk through this camp. He will see me. I'm sure his men have forgotten about me now."

Today, under a different citizenship and no contact with him family, Omar is still waiting for the day he and Ahmed can reunite. Ahmed may not even be living, but Omar says he feels in his heart that he is still alive.

"I hold onto my amulet," Omar says, fearfully clinging on to a supposedly-blessed amulet which protects Ahmed from afar, "and I feel him. I know he is alive. When peace comes, then I know where to find him. I know his village. I know his family names and even famous relatives of his. I will be able to find him."

saved by mogadishu

Like all young Somali people, Badal's parents expected him to get married and raise a family at a young age. When at twenty-two he still remained a bachelor, his mother traveled hundreds of miles south of Bosaso, where they lived, to find him a suitable wife in Galkacyo, where her family comes from and where she knew she could at least find one girl for her son.

"She didn't hide the fact that she was hunting for a wife for me," says Badal, now 28. "Of course, I was uncomfortable with the idea because I'm homosexual, but what could I have done? This was something everyone did. You got married on your own, or your parents, if you were lucky enough, found you a compatible person to begin your individual journey with."

However uncomfortable he was with the idea of getting married, Badal agreed to it when his mother returned with a beautiful young woman, five years younger than him. Suddenly, he was the hot shot in the neighborhood as all the guys wanted to take cues from him and his circle of friends seemed to have doubled.

"It was a strange experience," Badal remembers. "I was not popular at all. I mean, I had a few friends but because this girl was so beautiful every guy wanted to be my friend. I think a lot of these guys also thought that I was gay and once I got out of the situation, they could step in and take my place."

Most of these guys were the same ones who used to call him all sorts of names growing up, says Badal. They called him *lagaroone*, or incompetent, most of the time. But he was called many other things, including faggot. As a young boy, he was beaten a lot by these very men and was often excluded from activities because of his perceived weakness.

Badal says he "had a really sad childhood," adding, "I was feeling like an outsider in my own neighborhood—always walking around nervous. No one wanted to be around me, or be my friend. I was like a liability—if you hang with

me, you were not going to be allowed into any circles. So, everyone avoided me. It was horrible."

At the age of twenty-two, Badal was a virgin both to men and women. Up to this point, he had only fantasies about men.

"If I were straight, I would have had more action with the boys as they all had jerked off together because girls were off-limits," he jokes.

When the wedding day arrived he was as nervous, if not more, as the bride. In Somalia, brides are always nervous because they have to worry about having sex when they have gone through female circumcision and they know it will hurt. As a gay man, Badal also had his own fears. He remembers being soaking wet all day. No one gave attention because it was the beginning of the summer months when Bosaso is really hot.

In bed, however, things were different.

"She really liked me, I guess," he says, laughing. "She was all over me as soon as we got to the room. And this girl was really experienced, I'm sorry to point out. She was not a virgin at all. The funny thing is that outside the bedroom no one would ever imagine this 17-year-old conservative girl to be so wild and sexual. We had sex and it didn't hurt her one bit, and trust me I'm well endowed!"

If he hadn't decided he was gay by then, by the morning Badal was convinced he had no business being with women.

"I had no desire whatsoever," he says of his first night with a woman. "I could not wait for it to be over. And she was really into it, and I felt bad because I thought she should be with someone who was as excited about her as she was about me. So I relived all my crushes that night—just to make her happy."

A few days later, Badal told his family everything—that he was gay; that he could not be married to his cousin any longer; and that he wanted to just be celibate.

"I decided that if I can't be with women, then I will just not have sex with anyone. The possibility of being with a man in a relationship didn't cross my mind. I figured it can't work in my country."

His family was not really surprised, but they couldn't believe their son was telling them these things. His mother was not having any of it. She said that he was suffering from the work of the *Shaitan*, the Devil, and proposed that her son get some religious help. She took him to a sheikh who cured people of all sorts of illnesses. He had his compound in Qandala (Treanout), an ancient town about 65 miles east of Bosaso. This sheikh had a huge reputation for curing people of homosexuality.

"He was very creepy," Badal remembers. "He took one look at me and he wiggled his head. He said I could be cured of my homosexuality, and I wanted to believe so much that he could."

After several months of therapy that involved anything from the Qur'an being recited over him, sometimes for a whole day non-stop, to being beaten and to being forced to smell the smoke from all sorts of animal feces, Badal realized he was not going to change.

"I still had the same wet dreams, and same fantasies," he says. "Nothing was changing, not even a little. I was growing tired of all these stupid, unbearable so-called treatments. I was sick of it all. I was there for no reason. Inside me, I gave up."

One night, while everyone at the camp slept, he sneaked out. He called a friend of his in Mogadishu, and asked if he could stay with him for a while. When the friend agreed, Badal was on his way to Mogadishu the next day. He did not contact his family to tell them his plans.

"I figured the family would not understand," says Badal. "There was nothing for me in Bosaso but bad memories and shame. Before, it was just rumors and suspicions. Now surely everyone would know I'm homosexual, and I would face disgrace in my neighborhood. Why would I go there?"

Badal had never been in Mogadishu. Not before the civil war or after. And he had no idea what to expect. Bosaso was only affected by the war in a positive way as its population tripled because of the migration of those who consider it their ancestral homeland. Today, Bosaso is ten times a better city than before the civil war. Mogadishu, on the other hand, as Badal learned quickly, was another story.

"It was like a horrible sight," Badal remembers. "I got off the bus and I felt completely disoriented by the aura of war. I had never seen anything like that before. There were ruins and bullet holes and everyone looked like they were criminals. I was shocked."

A few days later, he called some friends in Europe and asked for a loan so he could go into business with Duran, his Mogadishu friend. When the people confirmed they would send money, he called his family to tell them that he is safe and living in Mogadishu.

When the money came, he invested with Duran and they opened two more stores in the *Bakaara* market, the largest in the city. Duran was in charge of the first store, Badal was in charge of one of the new stores and they asked a young man to manage the other and in exchange they would share the profits.

"His name was Mubarak," recalls Badal. "He was a Reer Xamar (Somali Arab) and very smart. Duran knew him from previous experience, and he felt Mubarak would help us grow fast. I was impressed by the way he spoke of business; it was as if he had a degree or something. It was great."

Not much after they opened businesses, Badal found himself in a different relationship with Mubarak.

"I was at the store he managed one night," remembers Badal. "And one thing led to another, and he kissed me. I have never been kissed before. Not like that! I felt like I was melting inside. We went to a hotel that night, and we pretty much made love all night long."

Weeks of love making later, Badal realized he was falling in love with Mubarak. This was particularly dangerous because aside from the fact that they were in business together, Mubarak was already married and had children. And Mubarak was honest from the beginning that he was not intending to have a relationship with a man and that this was nothing more than sexual. Much to Badal's surprise, Mubarak sat him down one night and told him that he was in love.

"I could not believe my ears," says Badal, laughing. "I was crying, he was crying. I told him I was already in love with him and, man, everything was beautiful—except we didn't know what to do. You know, what did this mean?"

They had no answer. Mubarak reiterated that he would not leave his wife and children. And there was Duran, who was straight, as far as they knew, and what about the business?

"I had a lot invested in the business, and I didn't want to lose it," Badal says, "but I wanted to be with Mubarak."

Also, there was the society to consider. Mogadishu was growing very conservative. Islamism was spreading, and everything was being monitored. There were Islamic courts, which afflicted people with all sorts of Sharia laws and regulations including laws for relationships. They were arresting, torturing and even executing people they felt were criminals including people who had sex outside of marriage. People were being chastised for silly things like watching television.

"We read stories in the newspapers of homosexuals being executed in Iran and Saudi Arabia," says Badal. "We knew it was possible in Mogadishu, and that was very scary. We decided to be low key, and avoid suspicion. Good thing is that not many people would suspect anything because we are business partners and it is natural we would be together a lot."

Badal knows that in a city like Mogadishu, haunted by strife, everyone is really busy with their own lives. Badal's fears have to do with the things he sees and knows rather than what others may see. In Mogadishu, it is not uncommon for men to be together. In fact, it is suspicious when they are not.

"And we are trying to keep an open mind about it," Badal adds.

Today, the two are still lovers a year and few months after they began their love affair. Mubarak stays a few nights with Badal, and fulfills his family obligations most of the week by spending the nights at his house, which leaves Badal feeling restless.

"He does tell me he wants to be with me," says Badal. "But it is hard. Every night he goes to his wife, I hurt even though I don't share that with him."

sakkwato lesbians must die

One morning, on her way to the local market, Hauwa was arrested. Under harsh conditions, she confessed to having carried out a love affair with a woman while she was married. While under arrest, her lover says, Hauwa was beaten and raped. But soon afterwards, she was executed. Her execution was unnoticed and unreported.

"It was not even discussed in the [local] newspaper," says Adia, the woman with whom Hauwa had the affair. "I didn't even know for days. This is how quick it was."

When she was sixteen, Hauwa's parents married her to a young man from their neighborhood. Soon, she was a mother. By the age of twenty-one, she had already three children. For a young woman who always struggled with her sexuality, she became deeply lost—leading to thoughts of suicide, as the pain was too much for her.

She had attempted to kill herself on several occasions. One time, recalls her lover, Hauwa had taken a lot of pills. But soon her mother-in-law realized she had taken something she wasn't supposed to as Hauwa struggled across the room with a seizure.

"The family put a lot of money into exorcism," remembers Adia. "There was nothing that could be done. No one knew why she was sad all the time. She would cry for days. Although no one was able to cure her, many Sheikhs said that the *Jinn* possessed her. The parents paid for many sheikhs to visit from all over the country. Nothing helped."

Adia, who was a young divorcee and a relative of Hauwa's husband, was called to help with the children as their mother deteriorated into depression. After being there for less than a week, Hauwa's mood has changed completely. All of the sudden, the woman was cured.

"The first day I arrived," remembers Adia, laughing, "I brought her lunch and she kissed me. I kissed her back. Well, that was the first day she finished her lunch!"

No one thought of anything about Hauwa's quick recovery, but the women began to fear. You see, around that time the whole northern states of Nigeria were becoming more and more *Sharia*-influenced. Within five years of the first state initiating Sharia laws, all of the sudden there were a dozen states ruled by Islamic laws. The hands of thieves were cut, adulterers were to be stoned, and all hell was breaking loose everywhere.

"We didn't know if there had been any lesbians arrested or killed," says Adia. "We listened to the radio and hoped to hear some judgment of what they thought. We heard of lesbians being executed in other countries with Islamic rulings such as Iran but never in Nigeria. Certainly, there were cases of male homosexuality but never heard of any lesbian ones."

One night, as Hauwa and Adia were making love, Hauwa's father-in-law came to the house. Although he did not see anything in particular, he was suspicious something was going on. Early next morning, he came back with his sons, two of which spied on the women as they slept. The women were in a spooning position, with Adia's hand between Hauwa's breasts.

"They rushed into the room," remembers Adia, "of course, we were scared. Then they all started beating me. They didn't do anything to Hauwa. At the time, I thought it was unfair because we were both guilty of what we did. But later I would understand she had it worse."

That day, Aida was taken back to the other city where she was from. She went through many beatings, and had to swear on the Qur'an that she would never repeat such behavior. As she immediately agreed, Adia was sent to an old Islamic shrine where she went through weeks of exorcism. And soon afterwards, she was given into marriage to a widower twice her age.

In the meantime, Hauwa's husband was consulted and he agreed to her being reported to the authorities. Because she was married, Hauwa's part in the affair was seen far greater sin in the eyes of the law. Her punishment was to be nothing less than an execution.

"I sometimes blame myself for what happened to her," says Adia, who is now miserable in a marriage she does not want to be in. "I wonder what would have happened if I never went there—would she still be alive? But sometimes I feel her spirit, and I'm happy."

To this day, Hauwa's family refuses to talk publicly about their daughter's case.

"What is there to say?" asks her mother, a frail woman looking a lot older than she actually is. "I feel pain in my heart, knowing I brought her to this world. She shamed herself, our community and myself. I would rather not speak her name, or remember her at all."

The local authorities no longer want to discuss the case either. The only person willing to even comment on the case is the judge. He is no longer involved with the authorities as he is retired, but took great pride in rejoicing his decision

"She had to die," says the judge, a man in his 70s. "*Sakkwato* [Sokoto] adulterers are sinners worthy of death. She confessed to lesbianism, during her marriage. So, therefore she had to die. We follow Islam, and we don't need to discuss cases like this."

mombasa masala

On the Swahili coast, Mombasa is known as the city that brings the world together. Since ancient times, African, Indian, Persian, Arab, Chinese and European traders all bring goods to the area through this city, in which the largest port of East Africa is located. And from it, they depart with some of the oldest treasures of the continent. Its citizens are a testament of this interaction: everyone in Mombasa can claim roots outside of its borders. They are people of diverse backgrounds.

In the 20th century, it also became a hot tourist spot for the adventurous and the guided travelers alike. On its beaches, the foreigners are sunbathing when they are not enjoying the warm Indian Ocean. Lovers of the sun from all over the world have accustomed to five-star service here.

In the middle of it all is Mousa, a 38-year-old gay man who owns a company that caters to the tourists.

"In this city one can find everything they want," he explains, "the Western traveler loves Mombasa because you can enjoy shopping like that of London or New York in the morning, but then can go to the beach in the afternoon and tan all you want. At night, you might want to go to a nightclub and dance until the morning. It is a fabulous life."

Mousa was born and raised in Eritrea. About five years ago, he was on vacation from Paris with his then boyfriend. Mousa was restless in Paris and, although he did not envision living in Mombasa, he did change his mind the last week before his boyfriend left for Mombasa.

"Philippe was coming here on business and persuaded me to come along," he says, laughing. "I had no idea how I would fall in love with this city. For me, as an African, it is a means to stay in Africa but still enjoy the diversity of Europe. Travelers here visit from all over the world. But we still must be careful because the laws are different here."

In Kenya, Sections 162 to 165 of the Penal Code illegalize homosexual relations and sets forth a punishment of up to 14 years in prison, aided by a

whopping 5 year term if one even attempts the crime. Mousa was used to a free Paris where gay rights have made great strides. Nevertheless, Mombasa intrigued Mousa. While he was here, he joked with his boyfriend that he would come back. Of course, his boyfriend didn't believe him.

"He laughed at me," says Mousa, showing a handsome picture of the man. "I remember how he said 'in Kenya, are you serious?' But I had no idea how serious I was. Being in Mombasa awoke something in me that I could not put my finger on let alone explain to someone else. I could not just tell Philippe how I really felt because it sounded so ludicrous."

When he went back to Paris, Mousa was haunted by the need to come back. He began to feel sadder as time went on and even saw a professional help. A few months later he broke up with his boyfriend, sold his apartment and came right back to live here. "There was such a pull to come back," Mousa remembers. "I did not know one person here. I mean, I had met some people on my visit but no one I would describe as a friend, and certainly no one I could rely to relocate. And the funny thing is that I didn't care. This was extremely out of character for me. All my life, I had been someone who lived by the rules. I had never been the kind of person to just pick up and move, even within Paris. I lived in the same apartment for many years. My friends are still shocked by all this."

As a predominantly Muslim city, gay life can be difficult here. On a typical evening, Mousa tries to incorporate much of his personal life into his business. He throws parties for his clients, and in turn his gay friends turn out to enjoy and to entertain themselves. He admits not all come for an innocent night out.

"In this city, every gay man wants to meet some Western rich boyfriend," he says, laughing, as his friend Abu dances across the room seducing the crowd. "It has never happened, at least not to my knowledge. But I can tell you one thing, there isn't a lack of trying!"

When Mousa moved to Mombasa, he immediately met Abu and Nasser at a resort famed for cruising. They are *Kutchi*—Kenyans of Indian background. They introduced him to Salim, an Arab gay man who was married with a wife and children at the time.

"The four of us are really close," says Mousa.

Abu is a 41-year-old dancer, and teaches all kinds of the art—including belly dancing, classical Indian, ballet and even hip-hop. Salim, 36, and Nasser,

32, on the other hand, are business partners in a successful local grocery store chain. Twice a week, these guys meet to catch up on all the latest happenings in their lives. They have created a sort of a circle, a family.

"We are always there for each other," says Mousa. "We all come from backgrounds where our families and larger Muslim community did not accept our homosexuality. Although we are all coming from different cultures and all speak different mother tongues, we are all compatible in our need to free ourselves. This is what makes us a unit."

And that they are.

When Nasser's mother died three year ago, they stayed with him for days—helping him to get through that extremely tough time. Nasser did not want to burden his friends, but they all chipped in with the funeral services and sort of shared the responsibilities of everything.

"I think it helped him a great deal to have that time with us," Mousa says. "When you lose someone that close, you want to be with people that you are also close to."

Likewise when a year later Abu's boyfriend of ten years left him for a younger man, the guys took him to Zanzibar for two weeks to get his mind off of the sad time.

"He just was broken," says Mousa. "But we were all there together."

In the same year, Mousa's ex-boyfriend was killed in a car accident back in France. The guys went to Paris with him for the funeral, and it was very difficult for them to get visas but they moved the earth and the sky to make it happen through committing all sorts of illegal activities.

"I have a lot of friends in Paris," says Mousa, "that was where my life was for many years. But I can't begin to tell you how amazing it was that these guys were with me there. I felt comforted by that fact alone. And because none of them have ever been to Paris, it was such a good distraction to play the tour guide. There would be moments when I didn't think about Philippe's death, and I don't think that would have been possible without them there."

Today, life is beautiful in Mombasa for Mousa. He says he even began to get the backbone to finally be able to visit his homeland of Eritrea, where a large number of his immediate family still live. And while he enjoys the memories of his childhood there, he always comes back to Mombasa because this is home now.

"There isn't any other city I would rather live," he says. "I'm very lucky."

casablanca beginnings

The first memory Masrah has of her early childhood is one where a woman teacher at the orphanage school beats her. She thinks she was about four years old. Not exactly the prettiest picture of childhood, and nothing good really follows.

Masrah was born in Morocco in the body of a boy in 1969. Nobody knows what city exactly. When she was an infant, she was found in front of a mosque in Casablanca. The imam was kind of enough to pick up the baby boy and take it to an orphanage house. The people there named the boy Muhammad, after the Muslim prophet who was an orphan. Masrah recalls the time she spent there as one full of sad moments.

"I had stayed in that place for twelve years," says Masrah, "I never remember any happy times. I remember some times when I was content. In my country, being an orphan is bad enough but I was also an orphan whose family no one had ever known, as well as a child who was very feminine and insisted on being a girl. I was faced with a lot of name-calling, including 'bastard,' 'faggot,' and many other horrible names used to humiliate people like me. I was constantly beaten, both by the authorities and the other children. It was a hard time."

Masrah says she did not have any role models. Everyone was either a boy or girl, and everyone she met had his or her respective genitals. For her, she was a girl trapped in the body of a boy. And there was nothing to compare it with. So at the young age of twelve, she ran away.

"I stole one of my [female] teacher's clothes," confesses Masrah, whose name means 'stage' in Arabic. "From that day forward, I wore women's clothes. Muhammad was put away and Masrah was born! I started performing when I was thirteen."

Performing, she means at weddings and other festivities where Masrah began to do belly dancing—especially the Egyptian style, which she learned from an aging dancer who took portions of her earnings in exchange for teaching her the craft. She struggled to make ends meet, and moved from one

set of whorehouse to another, even though she wasn't a prostitute yet but hang out with them for food and shelter.

When she turned fourteen, she met a Spanish man. He fell in love with her because she was everything a woman was… but without a vagina. "I was sharing hormones with a British friend, and I began to develop breasts," remembers Masrah. "And I had always had feminine features anyway, so by the time I was fourteen I really was like any other woman except that one part. He was sweet, and romantic. He was an easy soul to love."

Adriano, the Spanish guy, was straight but he did not care. He was taken by Masrah's personality. She was funny, and spoke an odd mixture of Spanish and Arabic with him—which more or less amused him. To him, Masrah was a confident, beautiful woman. He was head over heels in love with her. The only problem was that he came to Morocco with his company, and at the end of that summer he had to return to his country. Masrah could not go.

"So he went back," remembers Masrah. "And I was really devastated. I would joke with my friends before he left that I didn't care. After all, he was the one who was in love with me. But it turned out that I too was in love with him. Then a few months later, he was back. He got me some fraudulent documents and I was able to go with him to Madrid."

Being in Madrid proved to be a mixed blessing. On one hand, Masrah was the woman of a beautiful apartment she enjoyed. It was decorated with all the things she never had—a television, a surround system where she could enjoy the latest Arabic music in how it was made, and other simple things in life that were new to her. She was in control of her house. Her man would go to work in the morning, and would come home to a house completely Masrah's. And he loved it.

"I think he loved that I was submissive and dominant at the same time," she says, laughing. "I would do whatever he wanted but I also took initiative. This was not something he was accustomed to. He always faced Spanish women who either were too submissive or too dominant. And when he met Arab women in Morocco, they saw him as a white man and would be willing to give him everything. I was different from both, I guess."

On the other hand, Masrah grew up surrounded by people at all times. She had no idea how to enjoy being with herself. Although she was enrolled in several Spanish classes, she still found it mundane to be home by herself.

"I felt guilty," she says, "because here was someone who was changing his life for me. I'm not easy. Moroccan women are not easy to live with. There is a natural distrustfulness towards others, and especially towards the Europeans. We are always trying to rob them of every penny. You know, I would see all these women at the *souk* in Casablanca overcharging poor unsuspecting Europeans. This is the mentality there. And I felt guilty because I felt like those women. I felt like I was trying to extort more out of him."

But Adriano completely understood why she was bored. At first he introduced her to Spanish cinema, and even tried to get her to watch the soap operas. When he realized she needed more, he began to introduce her to a lot of his friends' wives. But Masrah was not used to these women, and was just as uncomfortable.

"I have to say that I always thought Spanish people have similar temperament as Moroccans," she says, laughing, "but I soon found out that was not the case. We Moroccans are wild but we are not vulgar. Spanish women are really vulgar and I just felt out of place with them. These women were calling their children all sorts of names. I was horrified."

But no matter what was going on, Masrah never forgot one thing. She was happy to be with Adriano. With him, she found some things that she never knew.

"There was a sense of home with him," she says, "even if boring, it was something usual and expected. I used to never know where I was going to sleep the next night. With Adriano, I had a home—a permanent place that was mine. And I don't mean this about a building; I mean the way I felt. His heart, and how I felt I belonged with him. I never had parents, and so I can't really speak what it is like to be the child of someone and to know there is someone who worries about you and does things in your name. This, to me, was Adriano."

For the first time in her life, Masrah found someone who wanted to genuinely take care of her. He loved her. She loved him. They became a family. Happiness finally introduced itself to Masrah. She and Adriano were settling into a comfort life.

"I had never known what it was to be happy," remembers Masrah, "this man gave me everything I had never even known existed. I remember sitting up at night in bed, while he slept away, and crying because I was so happy. I don't think I have ever been as attentive to anyone the way I was to Adriano."

After couple of years, Adriano began to be unfaithful. Masrah says he was looking for something she could not, biologically, provide. To return the favor, she began to prostitute. All of the sudden, she was all over Madrid. Her "exotic" looks attracted every guy. Some beat her when they found out she was a "man," others were okay with it. Within a year of prostitution, she saved up enough money to go to Asia (she refuses to disclose what country) and had her surgery.

"I came back a few months later as a whole woman," says Masrah. "Less than a week, Adriano asked me to marry him. I turned him down and moved back to Morocco. I just felt like he left me to dry when I needed him. I was the same person inside, why should a surgery change that?"

Still hurt over leaving the only man she has ever loved, Masrah began to change her life in Morocco. With two of her old friends from the brothels, she opened a restaurant in Marrakech. Much to her satisfaction, the restaurant became very successful after a few years. "A complete surprise," she says.

Over the years, Adriano came back to Morocco hoping to change her mind. But she never budged. She told him that it was a chapter in her life that she closed. "After all, I think he got the message. He stopped, and that was it," she recalls.

Today, the 35-year-old is a mother of two orphans she adopted from the same orphanage she grew up in. It was a struggle because the children were infants. She thinks she will adopt just one more. She continues to be single, but by choice.

"I'm just busy," she says. "Motherhood is busy enough but I'm also a businesswoman now. A very successful business, unfortunately, needs a very attentive owner. It really has been a dream come true. Who knew an orphan from Casablanca could be so successful in Marrakech? Perhaps when those guys named me after Prophet Muhammad, who became successful away from his birth city, they had some idea."

I bet.

the tehranian

As the capital of perhaps the most conservative government in the world, one is perhaps allowed to expect Tehran to be a town living in the dark ages. Instead, the city seem to be a contradiction between its past and future. The skyline is full of modern high-rises, some of which the designs leave you wondering what great architects are hostages here. And most unexpectedly, walking on its streets you run into women wearing the latest global fashion labels, adorned with make up, and who might recently have had varies plastic surgery performed on them.

At the same time, Tehran is the seat of the *Majles*—a nearly 300 legislative body that rule on everything, public and private, and who are determined to keep the Land of the Aryans an Islamic abode. And, because the secret police might just be around the corner, it's a city where everyone bites their tongue—lest they find themselves bruised, jailed or even executed.

But no one lives Tehran's contradictions more than Hossein. He is a 32-year-old gay man who spends many hours of the night in the city's underground—an almost invisible parallel world where sex might be free or for a small fee, drugs and alcohol are plentiful and where you might imagine being anywhere but in Iran. By day, however, Hossein assumes a conservative image that also oddly enough fits him perfectly. Walking into any governmental building, he seems part of the elite. And that, he is: his father is a revered and powerful ayatollah.

"I have a completely different life than that of my father," readily admits Hossein, however, adding, "and most people, including most of my immediate family, would be surprised to know I do some of the things that I do. My family is everything to me, but I'm definitely the bad sheep."

The family comes from a poor background but their luck had taken a better turn when Hossein was 5 in 1979 and the country fell into the hands of religion. Hossien is the oldest of several kids, and none of them remember the details of this period.

"We were all raised under the [Islamic] Revolution," recounts Hossein, who grew up in the north of the city. "I do remember feeling scared because my parents and everyone around me were anxious. Many of our neighbors moved out quietly. And suddenly everything in our country was drastically different. History was changing before our eyes."

By that time, his father had already mastered in *Shi'a* Islam and was on his way to becoming a respected leader in their local community. The father's fame, however, rose out of proportion when suddenly the country went from a more Western style hand into a strict Islamic interpretation. While Tehran's elite suffered a devastating loss, many of them leaving their beloved city behind, Ayatollah Khomeini's new government offered thousands of unknown men some prestigious jobs. Hossein's father was one them. Overnight, they went from poor to upper middle class.

"My father hates that we have money now," says Hossien, a graduate of Tehran University—the most respected and oldest university in the country. "He gives a lot of money to charities but mother makes sure he does not disrupt our lives. We have accustomed to a certain lifestyle now. If this was changed, some of us in the family would probably leave the country for Europe or America."

And this father won't have that.

Therefore, an unspoken deal was reached. In this deal, Hossein is allowed to have the kind of life he wants to have, but privately and away from anyone's judging eyes. In return, he must never set foot out of Iran. One would think this is a lot of pressure for a young man.

"This is a good deal," explains Hossein. "I do my part: even when high, I still show up for the Friday services at our mosque; no matter how late, I try to come home at night; when driving away in my BMW from the neighborhood, I play the Qur'an in my $1000 stereo imported from Germany. It may seem a hypocritical life to an outsider," he adds, with a grin, "but I consider this a give and take relationship. I couldn't have asked for a better life. When my cousins visited a few years ago from Europe, they were shocked. They said we live ten times better than they do over there."

On Keshavarz Boulevard, the largest and busiest street in the city, Hossein is sitting in traffic like millions of Tehranians everyday. Out of his tilt-mirrored sports car, burst the smoke from his imported Montecristo cigar. It is late Thursday afternoon and everyone is going home for the weekend. Unlike many, however, Hossein is on his way to join some gay friends—Morteza, Amir, and Sohrab—so they can prepare together for a hot party in the underworld later that night.

On the way, Hossein picks up Sohrab—a soft-spoken 33-year-old who closely resembles the American model/actor Antonio Sabato, Jr. Sobrab is Hossein's boyfriend of eight years. And to Hossein, there is no finer man.

"He makes me live everyday," says Hossein. "He is like my family because he loves me and worries about me. You know, in Iranian culture we value those who worry about us! Sometimes I would like for him to worry less but he is so good to me nevertheless. I wish I could be as loving as he is. It is the one person I continuously feel I fail. No one can match up to him."

They met as graduate students at Tehran University. They became good friends but only to fall in love less than a year later.

"I never fell in love before," says Hossein, laughing, "I could not resist him. I knew I was in trouble when I started to hurt every time I was away from him. He was not an ordinary friend; I realized I was falling deeper and deeper in love with him."

Once Sohrab felt comfortable, a sheltered Hossein was then introduced to Morteza—one of Sohrab's ex-boyfriends. Morteza, now 41, was then a young professor. Then Amir, one of Morteza's ex-boyfrineds, joined the group from Shiraz about a year after. Amir, now 38, had then just opened his own boutique. The four of them are now inseparable. "We just click," says Hossein.

In a conservative country like Iran, Hossein says the majority of new gay friends you meet are your friends' and lovers' former lovers and their lovers. Much of it he attributes to the laws against homosexuality, cultural stigma and the Iranian way of life.

"It is very hard to trust someone here, especially when telling them about your sexuality could mean the end of your life," explains Hossein, speaking from experiences, as he knows some people who have been arrested and died in jail. "Some gay guy will tell someone and that someone tells someone who knows a policeman and that policeman ends up arresting that someone. And you don't hear from them anymore. They stop coming to the functions.

Everybody knows what happened to them. So when you meet people you trust you must hold onto them."

This kind of system creates space for unusual relationships. Although Hossein and Sohrab have been together for these many years, they are not exclusive. Part of their understanding early on was that Hossein was going to get married, as he wanted to protect his family's name, and especially that of his father, but that as far as men go he and Sohrab would be boyfriends. To make matters a bit more complicated, Sohrab was already married with children. So he was no position to stop Hossein from wanting the same thing.

A few years after they met, Hossein agreed to an arranged marriage. No one was forced, and each of the young couple had his and her own secrets to protect. He was covering his socially detested homosexual relationship with Sohreb, his promiscuous cousin was already pregnant by one of her lovers. When she purposely swallowed the wrong pills to abort the baby, she knew Hossein would take her secrets to the grave.

"It was a great solution for both of us," recalls Hossein, of his marriage. "I still had a happy life while fulfilling my family's wishes, and she was avoiding a life of disappointment with her family. If her father knew the things she did, I'm very sure he would have killed her."

A year later, Hossein's wife died in a car accident. As the capital of a country with the highest fatality rate from crashes, accidents are accepted as part of life in Tehran. But the episode sent Hossein through a period of deep depression. He blamed himself.

"She reformed about her vice as soon as we got married," Hossein says. "I believed God was punishing me because I continued to have my relationship with Sohrab. I believed I was still living in sin. I was really suffering because I was torn inside. On one hand, I loved Sohrab deeply and couldn't imagine my life without him. On the other hand, I felt people I love would slowly disappear if I continued sinning. Then I decided to change."

Even though he thought he was not religious, the religious teachings of his father were catching up with him. Hossein pushed everyone away, especially Sohrab and their gay friends. When he couldn't deal with the pain, he turned to alcohol and drugs, formed new allies in different parts of the underworld and began a crime-infested life.

"Everything in my life was then disappearing," he says.

Sohrab never gave up. Day after day, says Hossein, Sohrab went after him and pleaded with him to stop. One day, Hossein listened. He moved in with Sohrab and his wife for a month and slowly came back to life. During this period, an interesting thing took place: Hossein got very close to Sohrab's wife. Oddly enough, she is still in the dark about her husband's sexuality as well as his long-term love affair with Hossein. Yet, none of that matters. Hossein is now very close to her.

"He jokes with me about her sometimes," says Hossein. "He will say things like 'Oh, you want to inherit my family!' or 'You want me out of the way!' because he knows that I would always be there for his family if anything ever happened to him. The wife is an amazing person. She did not resist helping me when perhaps I should never have been around any children. I have my life back partly because of her. These people forced me to see my life differently."

It is a little before midnight, and the boys are doing last minute cologne buffing and eyebrow straightening in Morteza's apartment in the Vanak—a formerly northern neighborhood that is now somewhat in the heart of the Tehran metro. Part of the evening was spent on catching up, gossiping over a delicious Italian dinner made by Amir and napping before getting ready. While the neighbors are already asleep, the night is still young where they are going.

"We don't do this everyday," injects Hossein, almost apologizing. "Maybe once every two weeks there is something big going on, and then we pull all stops! Really, it is a fun time." Looking over at Sohrab and Amir, who are completely dressed in drag, while Morteza sits with a mirror applying last-minute lipstick, Hossein adds: "And, of course, I never do that! There is gotta be a man in the car."

Farshid and Koorosh, a gay couple, have invited them to a party. It is taking place in Jonub-e Shahr, a neighborhood in the south—oddly enough where the city is most conservative. In the e-mail, the invitees were told Mahnaz—a male belly dancer who "borrowed" the name from a popular actress—will be making her appearance at 2 a.m. Since Mahnaz will be performing for many hours, with her long breaks and costume changes, it is expected hearts will race at least until daylight. Last time they were here—a few months earlier—they didn't leave until 8 a.m. the next day.

What does Hossein's family think of all this? "It is the weekend," he explains, changing to a serious tone. "They know I will go out to friends' house and have fun. I don't really think they know what I will be doing but they know I will be safe with Sohrab. You have to understand, my family and I are on a 'Don't Ask, Don't Tell' basis. In America, they come out to their families. In Iran, we live our lives without burdening anyone else because we don't think being gay is the center of life."

Like his three best friends, Hossein seems to be content with a double life full of secrets, contradictions, and dangers. And like a growing number of queer Iranians, he is carving his own identity in his own terms—whether others outside understand or not.

"First and foremost I am Hossein," he says, smiling. "I'm not going to let someone in New York or Paris tell me what I should be or how I should live my life. I may not march on the streets of London with a rainbow flag, but I can still enjoy my life."

Although he is very well versed in Western cultures (he can tell you everything you need to know about French art), and seems to know more about what is going on in Hollywood than many Americans (he subscribes to many online gossip and fashion magazines), he deeply cherishes his Persian culture.

When at 2 a.m. Mahnaz dashes out into the room with a favorite from the singer Googoosh, Hossein trances into the melody. While Mahnaz showcases his skills in Persian classical dance, Hossein slips slow kisses to Sohrab. It seems in Tehran, even if at 2 a.m., a romantic scene between men can always take place privately.

"For now," says Hossein, the next day, "that is good enough."

occupied hearts in palestine

The West Bank is an occupied territory in Palestine. It is an area that continued to be the subject of occupation since a little after its foundation in the Dark Ages. But more recently in history, it has become a rather political mayhem of sort. From 1948, when the State of Israel was created, to 1967, Jordan occupied it. And since 1967, Israel has continued to be its sole occupier. A whole generation has been born into that occupation.

Just six miles north of Jerusalem is a city called Ramallah. It is perhaps the center of Palestinian culture in the Middle East. Nineteen years ago, Rabiya was born here.

"Having been born into an occupation is not an easy time," says Rabiya. "It has been an extremely difficult life. I have cousins and other relatives in the West but they don't understand the horrors of living here. Growing up here, or even trying to love."

The constraints of the occupation are a strangely normal part of Rabiya's daily life. For example, to go to school and work, Rabiya must cross-checkpoints in and out of Jerusalem. Although the city is only fifteen-minute drive away, it takes her sometimes up to five hours.

"It's frustrating to face all these idiotic restrictions," says the 19-year-old History student, "but you get used to it. And after a while, it even becomes normal. I no longer get too upset when I have to wait hours just to be let go to school."

At home, Rabiya faces another kind of occupation. When a decade earlier the Israelis killed her father, it was her uncle who took the man's position and married her mother. Although this is not a common practice in the Palestinian culture (it is far more common in the Gulf), it does happen. While her father was an average Palestinian only worried about providing for his children, and not too much interested in religion, her uncle is an Islamist of sort.

"In order to live peacefully in my parents' house, I must cover up and not wear any pants or such," shares Rabiya. "But, of course, I don't keep that up.

As soon as I leave the area, I take it off. I'm not allowed to have any friends come over and he won't even let me be on the computer."

This gets even more complicated as Rabiya has been dating, for the past two years, an Arab lesbian who lives in Jerusalem. Not only does she have to hide her relationship with the woman but she also feels the need to keep the woman discreet altogether—not even introducing her as a friend, thinking that would invite more questions.

"I don't want to risk being found out," she reasons. "That would be the end of me. I'm not ready yet."

The two women work together at the library of the university Rabiya goes to. Outside of work, they don't have any time to be together. Rabiya says she wants to be with her lover but the circumstances are not allowing it for now.

"The biggest obstacle right now is that I can't leave because my mother is ill," says Rabiya. "She had been diagnosed with an illness I would rather not reveal. I pray that she will be alright. There is nothing I would love more than live with my lover and best friend, Leila. I just can't do it right now. I have other responsibilities, as she does."

Leila is working in Jerusalem to provide for herself and her parents, who live in Umm Al-Fahm—an Arab town in the Haifa District. Her only brother got into France illegally, where he works under the table but does not make enough to support himself.

"She ended up with taking care of the parents by herself," says Rabiya.

In the couple of years the two women were dating, they got to know other lesbian Arabs in the Jerusalem area. They have participated in couple of the pride parades, and also went to events at the Jerusalem Open House—the city's queer organization, which reaches out to the Arab community through its publications in the Arabic language as well as its Arabic section of their website.

"The combination of all these activities really do help a lot," says Rabiya. "When I talk to other lesbian Palestinians, although we hate the occupation at least we agree to be grateful for some of the relief we get in the open society of Israel. I know it sounds stupid but just holding Leila's hand when we are in a setting like the Open House makes me feel free. For a little bit, I forget all about the occupation. All the pain and suffering I face as a Palestinian, as a woman, as a lesbian."

leaving baghdad

In 2003, when the United States (and its allies) invaded Iraq and, within weeks, Baghdad fell to its invaders and chaos followed, Kemal, like millions of Iraqis, was hoping the country would be better after Saddam left. But that didn't happen. Instead, the country fell into a long, horrible state—caught between the West, who vowed to present a democratic and free Iraq to the world, and Iraqi insurgents, who saw the West as occupying forces who came to steal their wealth.

"My friends and I were waiting for the freedom," says Kemal, a 33-year-old gay man. "Instead, we ended up feeling like we were in the tenth century. We had no water for months. We couldn't go outside because there were all these bombs taking off between the Americans and the Islamists. It was absolutely horrible. We felt like we lived in the battlefronts. We did live in the battlefronts. We just didn't know it was that."

Like most Iraqis, Kemal has seen his life change drastically. Before the invasion, he had a relatively quiet life. About ten years earlier, after the first Gulf War, Kemal moved from Najaf, a city about 90 miles south of Baghdad. He had been dating a wealthy man who lived in Al Mansour, Baghdad's wealthiest district. He was just twenty-one, and was fleeing the pressures of his extremely religious Shi'ite family to get married.

"Ali [the lover] was very hospitable," remembers Kemal. "We never had sex before I decided to move to Baghdad, we just communicated through phone and letters. I told him I wanted to come because my father was in late stages of fixing me in a marriage. Anyway, when I came to his house, Ali didn't pressure me. I lived with him for months before we had sex. This made me feel very safe, something I hadn't felt all my life because I was gay in a religious neighborhood in Najaf."

For the first time in his life, Kemal lived a romantic life—something he had dreamed of for many years. Ali took him to the best restaurants in the

city where they would have special table or sometimes the entire restaurant—with candlelights, imported drinks and the works. They mingled amongst the richest in the social clubs of Baghdad. They vacationed exotic places all over the world—flying private and staying at luxurious resorts. He learned how to drive, and was totted in the most expensive cars in the world—some of which he had never heard of. He was given access to bank accounts with more money than he ever thought was possible in one person's possession.

Ali introduced Kemal to the West—the arts, the culture and history. He taught Kemal English and French simultaneously with private tutors from some of the respected professors of the languages, as well as taking long vacations in countries like France, England, Canada and the United States. Within a year, gifted Kemal could speak these languages better than some locals. And Kemal took the opportunity, and divided into the cultures of these languages where vacationed alone when Ali was working.

And all of this took a toll on him.

"Ali was forty-five, and he was a great man, but I felt bored with him," remembers Kemal. "So I began to have affairs with other young gays. And, of course, I was introduced to drugs and all that. I saw myself change. Ali had no idea what was happening to me. I was not coming home sometimes for days. He really loved me but he thought I was becoming too dangerous for my own good."

Ali kicked Kemal out of his house and cut him off from all financial dependency. Now that he had no bank accounts with lots of dough, Kemal had seen Baghdad for the first time for what it was—a capital fueled by greed, corruption and persecution. One night, after leaving a party really late with some guys, he was arrested.

"I was high on drugs," says Kemal. "I don't even remember why they stopped us but I guess they noticed we were all on drugs. In jail, the guards as well as other inmates raped me repeatedly. I made a decision in that prison to change my life."

When he came out, Kemal cut off all of his "friends." Since it had been more than a year, Ali had already taken another lover. There was no point in going back to him. He had to find other sources to stay cool. Because he spoke English so well, and was clearly a charming person with a lot of personality, he found a job with an NGO.

"I did all their international begging," he says, as he laughs. "I was making good money because I was able to solicit a lot of money from varies charities and foundations in different countries. Every time I got money for the organization I was paid a percentage on top of my regular salary, which was nothing honestly."

Slowly, Kemal's life came back to some sort of normalcy. He rented a flat in Zayuna, the city's "gay" neighborhood, bought a car, and began to become friends with some nice gay guys who did not do drugs or drink too much alcohol. Even Ali came back as a friend.

"I really had a good, stable life," remembers Kemal. "It was work, have fun, and lived my life without any stress. I met varies guys as lovers and although none of them worked out I still was happy with my life."

Then began the rumors that the United States was going to attack Iraq. Almost everyone in his "well to do" circle left the country. Soon, it was just him and two other friends left in Baghdad. And the closer the invasion got, the more Kemal questioned his reasons to stay behind. But he loved Baghdad, and although he traveled elsewhere in the Arab world, he didn't find somewhere else he thought he could live. Then came that dreaded day. The West was dropping bombs in Baghdad.

"And everything changed," remembers Kemal. "I could not even get money out of my bank account. It was as if we were hijacked by aliens. That summer was the worst summer of my life. It was just horrible everywhere. In Baghdad, it was as if we were witnessing the end of days. So many people got killed."

But all that time, Kemal was suffering just as any other Iraqi. However, after the invasion the lives of gay and lesbian people in Iraq changed specifically. As the country fell more and more into chaos, a lot of young gays became sex workers. It was an easy way to make money. But this got dangerous. All of the sudden, some of these people started disappearing.

"At first, we thought they stopped," says Kemal, some of whose friends were in the business. "But they were not anywhere to be found. Then we thought perhaps they are leaving the country. Of course, then we realized the awful truth: they were being kidnapped, and murdered out of sight."

In October 2005, these murderers no longer had to kill gays in secret. Grand Ayatollah Ali al Sistani, perhaps the most revered Shi'ite cleric in Iraq, released a *fatwa* ruling that homosexuality is illegal and that gays should be punished, killed. This led to widespread killings of gays throughout the country.

"The first time I realized this was bigger than I thought was when they killed Hussayn," Kemal remembers. "He was a very sweet, and gentle person from Najaf. Everyone knew he was gay because he was very feminine. One night, as he slept, someone came into his room and shot him in the head. They left a note saying he should not be buried but burned."

As he was mourning the loss of his friend, Kemal heard of other killings in Baghdad. One of them he knew very well. It was the boyfriend of one of his friends who left Iraq. The man couldn't go with his boyfriend because his mother, who was in her 70s and ill, refused to leave with him. He wanted to bury his mother before he went anywhere. Now it was his old mother who had to bury him.

"Everyday, we heard someone got killed here or there," says Kemal. "A lot of the people who were sex workers got killed. Gay men who were out were killed. It was happening so often. We had to hide."

Kemal, who had been wering designer clothes, changed the way he looked. He bought some religious clothes, and stopped wearing anything that might identify him not just as gay but someone who is familiar with the West, which was just as dangerous because the insurgents then would think one is an informer for the Americans. He stopped listening to Western music, or he would listen with headphones. He completely stopped meeting other gays. All of the sudden, he was living in fear.

"I said to myself 'this is not the Baghdad I want to live,'" he remembers. "I loved this city. I have the best memories of my life here. I never thought I wanted to leave. Even Paris or London did not attract me more than Baghdad. But after seeing what happened to my friends, and to gays I didn't even know, I thought it was pointless."

So he called up Ali in Dubai and asked to join him.

Today, Kemal lives with Ali and his boyfriend. He admits he misses Baghdad and would love to live there again, but not until all these horrible things stop. He says he won't go there until the West leaves, and the country goes back to a place he can be proud of.

from lebanon, with love

Fatma grew up in a tiny house just behind a church in Lebanon. Her family was very religious. She clearly remembers her father cursing the church whenever the bells rang.

"'May Allah take them!' he would say something like that," she recalls. "So I really grew up in a fundamentalist household. I knew from a young age—as young as five—that it was not allowed for me to be just any Lebanese but was required to be a Muslim Lebanese."

Like many Muslim girls in the Arab World, she says, she was expected to live a certain life: get some form of basic education in Islam and in general, get married, have many children and help those children with that basic education.

"Everything was laid out by my family history," she says, staring at a wall full of old pictures. "The women on my father's side of the family just never do anything important with their lives. I mean, my aunts are all slaves to their husbands and children. They didn't lead the kinds of lives I would look up to but I had no choice."

When she was seventeen, her father married her off to a man more than twice her age.

"It was a very difficult situation to agree to at first because I knew I was a lesbian," she says, with tears in her eyes. "It wasn't something I thought might be a problem. I thought, 'I can always fake it.' After all, I knew many of the women in my family were not sexually satisfied anyway."

For Fatma, marriage could prove to be an opportunity in itself.

"It would be the first time I would have gained some sort of freedom over my life," she says. "I imagined a life away from my father for so long. And although I was a lesbian I knew my only way out was through marriage. I know that sounds contradictive, but it really is true. So I agreed to the marriage with the intention that I would have a separate life from my family."

Fatma suspects her husband, who was thirty-eight when the couple married, a man who spent many years abroad in France, was a closeted homosexual.

"He did not care much for a romantic life with me," she remembers, laughing. "He did have sex with me on certain occasions but he was clearly not interested. And when I would tell him I didn't feel like it, which was most of the time anyway, he would never push."

And, of course, they had some things in common.

"He, too, came from a religious family," says Fatma. "So, of course, it was clear a life without marrying was not an option for him, either. In the privacy of our home, we both lived the kind of life we wanted, I think, even if that did not entail sexual happiness."

To give her more freedom, Fatma's husband spent a lot of time away from home. He traveled to Europe often, says Fatma.

"He was probably cheating with men, but I didn't care. It was the best thing ever. Why would I question him about something that was helping me? I let him stay in Europe or America for as long as he wanted to stay."

Although marriage was not exactly the best thing in the world, Fatma needed something out of the marriage; children. But the universe had other plans.

"I could not get pregnant," she says. "We tried for the first couple of years without success. I was beginning to think it had to do with me and my sexuality. But after I talked to doctors, they told me it was not because of my lesbian feelings."

She got pregnant three years into the marriage. Fatma says she wanted children because it was something programmed in her by her family.

"I was very close to my mother," she says of her mother who died from diabetes. "I wanted to have children of my own. I wanted to have that kind of love with them. The kind of emotional connection I had with my mother. Regardless of always feeling some sort of an alien in my family, it was that connection with mom that gave me purpose."

Fatma lost the baby, and she never got pregnant again.

"I actually began to push him to have sex with me after my failed pregnancy," she remembers. "I wanted to have a child so bad and I internally blamed myself because he was excited about having a child. Having sex with him was repulsive but the need for a child was greater for me."

One summer, her husband went to Europe and he just never came back. He never called. Nothing. Worried, Fatma began to investigate.

"I phoned his friends in Paris," she says, "but they didn't know where he was. Then one night I got a very disturbing phone call from his mother. She said her son wanted to divorce me because I was not giving him any children. Since she controlled every aspect of his life, I did not see any reason to argue with her."

His mother asked Fatma to think about it, and she did.

"I thought it would be very good if I could leave the country, somehow," she says. "I did not want to go back to my father's house because it would dishonor him in the eyes of the family. But I just really did not want to be under my father again. No way! So I asked that in the divorce. I would do it but if they only didn't tell my father."

The husband helped Fatma to get into France where they divorced quietly.

"We never kept in touch," she says, "so I don't know where he is today. My father never knew because he died a few years later. My sisters and brother all know now but it is old news. They keep it from the extended family, and that is okay."

Today, strangely enough, Fatma is married to an Algerian man with whom she has children and travels back and forth between his home country and France.

"I still wanted children," she says, laughing. "I learned the problem of the difficulties of getting pregnant was actually with my ex-husband, because as soon as I got married to my current husband I conceived a child right away."

But aren't there other way of having children?

"I was never going to be one of those western women having children the wrong way," she says, as she laughs. "Besides, he is a good man. He knows who I'm and he is willing to live with it. We try very hard to have a life happy to both of us."

The "wrong" way she is referring to here is the artificial insemination many doctors recommended for her before she remarried. Fatma says it never was an option.

"I think it is unhealthy for children to grow up in such homes," she says. "I have a happy life now because it is on my own terms. I decided. Why bring children into the world if you cannot afford to give them a home of two parents?"

I ask if she ever wishes she were with a woman instead.

"Of course, I do," she says, "but I would miss a lot more if I were with a woman. I would be unhappy to be waking up with a woman every morning, with an empty house. It is not my way of life or how I see life should be for me. It is not me."

Does she ever enjoy the sex? No, she says. "It is something to do, a chore, just like cleaning your house or something like that. Some people like to clean house, others will not like it the same. I love my husband but it is not romantic love. It is the love of a brother, a dear friend. It is better."

What really is surprising the most about Fatma's story is her husband's acceptance of her sexuality although he is a practicing Muslim.

"Well, because I can give him everything he wants in a wife," says Fatma. "Not many women of today will be obedient, faithful and elegant wife at the same time. He loves me because I'm his ideal wife. To everyone outside of our bedroom, we are THE couple. His male friends envy him. We don't look at marriage the same way people in the West do."

So is Fatma doing all this for children, and if so, why is she then condemning the women of her family for the same thing? "No, of course not, it is not just for children," she says, "it is just partly for children. It is also part of my whole picture of what a good woman is. What I don't like about the women of my family is that they never decided. It was decided for them. I decide what I do in my life. I live in Paris where I can find a suitable woman to be with. I met my husband on my own. He is not even from the same country as I'm. So I decided."

Interesting, indeed.

learning to live in cairo

Rashid was born as a girl to an Egyptian couple in midtown Cairo. He was named Rashida, the female version of the name Rashid. As early as five, Rashid remembers having an impulse against his physical gender. When his parents dressed him in skirts, he hid in his brothers' room and changed into their clothes—facing physical abuse from them for "degrading" their clothes.

In the early teenage years, when girls began having sexual feelings for the boys, Rashid's mind was confused by the fact that he too was actually attracted to boys. Did this mean he was a "normal" girl? Did this mean he was a tomboy who was a girl underneath it all? Was something seriously wrong with his psyche? These were some of the questions that constantly haunted him.

"It was one thing to like boys' clothes and toys," says the now 42-year-old Rashid. "It was quite another to like them sexually. It didn't make sense to me in my head. You know, the males that I knew did not have sexual feelings for one another. Men did not marry each other. I started to think maybe I was a confused girl. However, my feelings that I was a boy did not change. It was a very confusing time in my life."

On the surface everything was fine, says Rashid. He was attracted to boys, and the boys were attracted to this beautiful body of a girl. Internally, Rashid was in pain because he was dealing with all these gender questions as well.

"It was a conflicting world," he says of the experience. "Just thinking about it brings tears to my eyes because I really was a lost soul at that time. My world was perfect to everyone except I was in pain and struggling to figure out how it all made sense."

In a conservative society as that of Egypt, it was difficult to talk about these issues with family or friends. Instead, Rashid began a quest to discover himself. One summer while vacationing in southern Egypt with family, he became sexually active with a cousin. The cousin enjoyed Rashid's body but

Rashid was not having any fun. When Rashid explored his sexual fantasies, the cousin was turned off by the experience.

"I wanted to mount him instead of him mounting me," says Rashid, laughing. "Since I didn't have a penis to do so, the only thing I could think of was be in control. He must have thought I was a slut when I jumped on top of him and took control of his lips and held my hands both sides of his cheeks."

Years of suffering later, the puzzle finally started to fit when Rashid saw a homosexual pornography film from Europe. Here were two beautiful young men sexually pleasing each other—one mounting the other in perfect harmony.

"It dawned on me," remembers Rashid. "Not only was I male inside but I was a homosexual male! This was a great breakthrough for me. That night I cried for many hours."

Rashid says he cried because he felt he lost so much time in discovering who he is. Today, however, he feels it was the perfect age. Rashid was nineteen when he made the connection. A year later when his father put him up for an arranged marriage, Rashid considered it, thinking he might find a gay man in the process but he found out the proposed man was heterosexual. Rashid then left the country for Kenya where a friend of his lived.

"Kenya was very cool country," remembers Rashid. "My friend Shoukri lived in the heart of Nairobi and I fell in love with the city immensely and immediately! I should have been sad and depressed that I left my whole life in Egypt but I really was not. I was actually happy for the first time in my life."

After living in Nairobi for many years, Rashid met a woman from England. The two became good friends and this led to Rashid's interest in London. He heard so many stories about transsexuals there that he decided to move to London at the age of twenty-five. A friend of his British friend brought him as a "wife."

In London, Rashid found friends who were gay and lesbian. Slowly, his understanding of himself grew. This also extended to other ways in his life.

"I went to school to become an interior designer," he says, showing me his degree. "It took a lot of work, but I did it. I was able to persevere because I no longer had that shadow in my life. I was making decisions based on what I wanted to do, not for family or anyone else. And it was loads of fun!"

Today, although he has not yet had the surgery that would complete his body, he still lives his life and identifies as a gay man. But Rashid admits it is not easy.

"It is tough to live any life," says Rashid. "My particular problem is that I'm having a hard time meeting gay men who are interested in a man with a woman's body, but I'm growing to be okay with the idea of being single. And, honestly, I have a lot to be thankful for. I could have been married in Egypt with kids and life I did not want. I can't imagine what life is there for those like me."

Rashid learned ways to go back to Egypt. About four or five years ago, Rashid met a a man who became a friend and a client as he was building a home in Cairo—choosing Rashid to do the interior design.

"This was a very wealthy man," says Rashid. "He paid me very well, and I was able to enjoy life in Cairo in ways I didn't think were possible. With money, I found Cairo to be a different city, I have to say. Even the authorities treat you differently."

Seeing the opportunity, Rashid bought a luxury apartment there. He rents it most of the year, but for the majority of the winter, he goes there.

"It gives me a way to get out of the cold European atmosphere," he says. "And I must say I really, really love Egypt now."

stolen moments in shiraz

It is early Friday morning, and Massoumeh is hurrying back home before her husband gets upset. After she made and served breakfast, she had to run to a store to buy some things to prepare his favorite lunch later—*chelo kebob*, a popular Iranian grilled meat (of any kind), served with saffron-flavored basmati rice, which her husband likes to eat nice and hot right after he gets home from the Friday prayers at the mosque.

If he sounds a bit demanding, he is.

"He won't eat anything else," complains Massoumeh, a 33-year-old wife and mother of three. "He doesn't even care to know what I or the children want. He wants the same thing, cooked the same way, on every Friday. I have no choice but to listen to him."

A few weeks earlier, when Massoumeh defied her husband on the occasion of her son's birthday and cooked the son's favorite food instead, she says he beat her so hard she ended up in the hospital. "I had bruises all over that I could not leave the house for days," she adds.

The other side of town, Nahit is struggling to decide what to eat for breakfast. Her husband had been out all night with his friends—playing cards, drinking and God knows what else. He only came home after sunrise. Unlike Massoumeh, she is on her own as far as breakfast and lunch go. Nahit and her husband are both Jewish, but he neither observes the Sabbath nor cares for what day of the week it is. So instead of cooking, she eats some oatmeal and heads to Massoumeh's house. "He does this all the time! What can I do? I have no control over him," complains Nahit, a 28-year-old who is pregnant for the first time. "I still need to eat because of my child. Before this [pregnancy], I used to eat whenever I go over to Massoumeh and we would share a meal like loving people should. But now I must eat on certain times of the day."

The two women are lovers. Seven years ago, they met when Massoumeh responded to an Internet ad posted by Nahit on a small Persian list for lesbians

moderated from Los Angeles. At the time, the then 21-year-old Nahit was to be given in marriage. Freaking out of the prospect of spending the rest of her life with a man, she posted a little cry for help. Meanwhile, Massoumeh had given birth to her second child and was falling into a life she did not want.

"We carried a very gentle friendship at first," says Nahit, "I wanted to go faster but Massoumeh was not up to it because she had a problem with having a Jewish lover. But over the years, it has indeed developed into a sweet, meaningful relationship."

In a country where most queers don't even identify as gay or lesbian, it is truly amazing to hear these women refer to their relationship for what it is. "But it has taken us some years to get to this point," explains Nahit. "At first, it was hard for me to accept I'm a lesbian—even when I was on a lesbian chat list. And we are still struggling because we live on stolen moments."

This morning, Massoumeh knows Nahit is on her way. And she is praying Farid, her husband, will be gone by the time she gets here. If she is lucky, he will decide to go to the mosque and read a few portions of the Qur'an there before the service. "He always starts questioning me why I have people visiting. I don't want him to suspect anything," she says.

During the working weekdays, which in Iran are from Saturday through Wednesday, they don't have this problem. Farid works as a Civil Engineer. He is gone most of the day; from early morning until evening. Sharokh, Nihat's husband, owns a shop in a local bazaar (mall). Sometimes, Sharokh leaves early in the morning as well and doesn't come home at all until a day or two later.

"While they are at work, and the children are at school, it gives us sometime to be together," says Massoumeh. "My oldest is nine. And she is beginning to be at that age when they understand things, and I don't want to risk anything."

Massoumeh is freaking out because she certain if her husband discovers about the relationship she has with Nahit, he will expose her to the government and that she, along with the love of her life, will face humiliation, jail time and ultimately be executed in public.

"It really does happen a lot in Iran," explains Massoumeh, "I think people don't know this outside of this country. There are many executions every day. Heterosexual adulterers, men and women accused of homosexuality and all sorts of other people that the government finds offenders of many idiotic laws. I'm scared all the time, but not Nahit. She thinks nobody cares. 'As long as we keep our husbands, everything will be fine,' she always says but that is not true. The fact that we are both married women—we will be stoned to death."

Nahit, on the other hand, feels their relationship is worth the risks. "I just don't have fears because I know what our married life is like," confesses Nahit. "I'm married to an absent husband, who spends the nights away from me, abandoning me in cold bed by myself while he keeps whores with himself in the store. And Massoumeh is married to a monster that beats her up everyday for the littlest things imaginable. It is amazing, truly. This is a man who prays five times a day to God, and yet if his wife irons his shirt the wrong way he beats her. So, we would be dead without each other anyway. Are we going to be exposed? I don't care. Let them expose us."

Not today. Farid decides to leave for the mosque early with his seven-year-old son. Massoumeh, her nine-year-old daughter and four-year-old son are left in the house. Only twenty-five minutes after he leaves, Nahit gets there. The two women are happy to be alone for a few hours together. Now, all they have to worry about is getting that chelo kebab ready for Farid.

somewhere in hijaz

According to friends, Amr was born in 1961 in Jeddah's old town, Al Balad. The City of Eve, as many believe the matriarch was buried there, Jeddah has always been a modern side of Saudi Arabia. His family wealthy and privileged, he spent many summers in Europe and Australia. During the holidays, he would spend time in his family's private château in south of France with Asian nannies, drivers and caretakers, who tended to his every need ... while his parents partied in south Florida. Amr received a high class, western-style in-home schooling. His teachers included two who held PhDs in Sociology and Philosophy. Amr should have been the poster child for modern Arab excellence.

But Amr was troubled.

He was haunted by memories of being sexually abused by his uncle at the age of five. At the tender age of eight, one of his former teachers molested him. And by the age of ten, he was having "consensual" sex with his family's drivers—men twice or three times his age.

"He was addicted to sex," remembers Tareq, a childhood gay friend. "The early and mid 1980s were the hardest. I was always so afraid he would catch AIDS."

Amr didn't catch any diseases but deeply struggled with depression. Tareq and other friends remember how he was depressed most of his life. A small family by Saudi standards, Amr grew up in a family of four—with his older brother and parents. He spent most of his life away from his parents—who did not spend much time in the house, and traveled extensively abroad. His brother, ten years his senior, did not want to hang out with him because he felt Amr was too young for him. Amr was left with a house full of workers—from spoiled female nannies to physically and sexually abusive male teachers and drivers.

In 1988, at the young age of twenty-two, Amr met a British journalist named Matthew. For the first time in his life, Amr fell in love—and rather

quickly. Matthew was everything Amr desired; tall, blond and blue-eyed English gentleman. Matthew was twenty-one years older, and in that Amr found both a lover and a father. Amr was swept off of his feet. It would last forever, he believed. Then after a few months came the bad news. One morning after a long night of lovemaking Amr answered the hotel phone while Matthew was in the shower. It was a woman. It came out that Matthew was married with three children and had no intention of ever leaving his wife and family.

Amr was devastated.

"Everything in his life broke down," recalls Tareq. "I remember him crying for hours and hours until there were no more tears in his eyes. He told me his heart was bleeding inside, and that he wanted to die but was too afraid to commit suicide."

Torn between the misery of the world and fear of hellfire in the world to come if he committed suicide, Amr withdrew from everything he knew.

"Slowly he became an empty soul," says Tareq. "None of us really knew how to help him overcome his sadness. It was a big loss, and we just did not understand it."

Matthew went back to London while Amr fell into a life of drugs and alcohol. He stole a lot of money from his family, left Saudi Arabia and strayed left and right in the streets of Rio de Janeiro. He was having sex with strangers as many as ten times a day. He was beaten twice—with one time so serious he ended up in the hospital. A few months later, his brother found him and brought him back home. Everyone was so shocked at how horrible Amr looked. He lost so much weight that many did not recognize him. He had missing teeth, his hair fell off and his skin became something ancient.

"We were all so happy to know he was alive because he cut off from everyone," Tareq says. "[His brother] Abdallah saved his life by bringing him back. Although many of us never liked Abdallah before, that act somehow redeemed him in our eyes. We became so grateful to him. Blood runs thick."

The family didn't care about the money, says Tareq. They were happy to have their son back. But Amr was not happy to be back. After a while, with psychological help, he began to accept his loss and decided to make the best of his life. He decided to go to university in America to earn a degree in English. He wanted to be a writer, he said. His friends and family were happy that he took a positive turn and they decided to support him. Less than a year later, he was accepted into a university in Florida where his brother lived. But not before kicking the drug habit and ultimately putting the bottle away. Everything was well again.

A few years later, Amr got his degree. And during that time, he worked very hard to remain celibate. At twenty-seven, his family married him to a cousin from back home. She was educated in the west and opted for a dual life at home and in America.

At this point, Amr "really believed he was able to overcome his homosexuality," Tareq recounts. "Those of us who knew him very well doubted this but it was something he truly believed he achieved. I was happy he was no longer exposed to diseases the way he was before. Deep down, however, I knew something was not right."

Less than six months of married life, Amr expressed to friends like Tareq that he was deeply unhappy. His wife, who was a very nice woman, was not what he desired, Amr confessed. So he decided to give up life in America—where he thought his "fantasies" were supported by the many blonds and blue-eyed men—and became a full-time Saudi resident. Perhaps this would work, he thought.

It didn't.

While still married, Amr met Ben—a Jewish archeologist student from America. Interestingly enough, Ben was neither blond nor blue-eyed. But the sexy dark-haired and green-eyed Jewish man made a lasting impression on Amr while the two were waiting at a doctor's office in Jeddah.

"They just talked," says Tareq. "They exchanged contact information and that was it. Amr came home and would not stop talking about Ben. It was just like that. We thought it was not going to be serious because Amr was already in marriage, and we knew Amr was not the kind of person who was unfaithful."

Although very resistant, Amr fell in love with Ben. This time around, the man was not married and interested very much in committing to Amr. However, Amr was at loss because he did not want to "disgrace" his cousin by divorcing her. And to make matters worse, she got pregnant as the men were discussing where they stand.

Amr and Ben agreed on continuing to be together. Amr would lead a double life, and Ben would just have to be content with stolen moments. But the longer they were together, the more and more Amr was with Ben and away from his wife and child.

"This continued for several years," remembers Tareq.

After a while, it became a common knowledge to everyone in Amr's life—including his wife—that Amr was with Ben for good. Jealous and feeling betrayed, Amr's wife moved away to Britain, the one country she knew Amr hated although she never understood why. If he resisted the move, she "vowed to tell his parents about his sexuality and demand a divorce," Tareq recalls.

In the meantime, Ben was offered a teaching job in America. He took it. Amr was now spending most of his time in the United States, only visiting his wife two to three times a year. While he never did anything with his English degree, he continued to write journals about his life.

"He knew I was the safest person to keep them with," says Tareq, who moved to southern California with his then boyfriend. "I loved Amr like a brother and I never judged his life in anyway. Somehow he trusted me the most out of our friends."

More and more, Amr was growing weary of the pressures from his family who demanded he spend more time with his child and wife. Finally, in 1993, he came out to them. "To say they were angry would not explain how they felt," says Tareq. "Especially his mother, she never talked to him after he came out."

Well, the family immediately cut him off. Although he had a lot of money saved up and invested outside of Saudi Arabia, the then 32-year-old Amr was on his own for the first time in his life. Tareq remembers Amr growing more depressed quickly. The abandonment of his mother, whom he was close to, was what hurt the most. Ben was at loss because he saw Amr's family as progressive, modern people who could overcome anything cultural or religious thanks to Amr's romanticizing his family over the years.

Everything turned sour when Abdallah vowed to kill Amr after their father promised either him or Amr would have to die, and that they could not share a life on this earth. Ben and Amr had to start living as quietly as possible. They moved out of their prime Manhattan apartment, Ben quit his job and the couple resettled outside of San Francisco.

"They were not living in fear," remembers Tareq, "but they were being very cautious."

Without Ben's income, the couple now had to rely solely on Amr's savings. So they decided to be proactive. They opened a small designer's boutique in a mall in San Francisco. Then in early 1994, they opened a deli in San Jose. Neither of them could tend any of the businesses, and Ben quickly grew dissatisfied with a life of being idle.

"He wanted to do something," says Tareq. "Ben was never the kind of person happy with not doing anything all day. It frustrated him."

In the meantime, Amr stayed a whole year away from his wife and child. And she took a great advantage of this. She met a Moroccan-born Dutch student at Oxford, and became extremely happy with him. Tareq says they had a child out of wedlock, which the families assumed was Amr's. At the two ends of the world, it seemed a married couple was living a happy life … but only with other people.

Amr continued to make life work with Ben. The couple continued to live in hiding. In late 1995, Ben finally had it. He broke up with Amr and went back to New York. He said he did not bargain for a life filled with hatred and fear, and that no matter how much he loved Amr he was just not willing to live like that. Then after couple of months, the couple reunited. But on Ben's terms. They kept their businesses in California but Amr moved back to New York. Ben started working again. And, most hard to overcome, Ben demanded that Amr divorce his wife.

By this time, the family gave up going after Amr. Things somewhat cooled down but there was no contact between the family and Amr. He divorced his wife against her wishes because she knew her family would expect her to move back to Saudi Arabia if she was divorced, which would force her to give up her Moroccan boyfriend.

Tareq says the year 1996 was the happiest year of Amr's entire life. He turned thirty-five and, for the first time in his life, was living a life he was proud of. He was living for himself. He sold the businesses in California, and opened a far-out gallery in the heart of Manhattan. Everything was finally good.

Then, for no apparent reason, Amr began to really go down. He became extremely depressed in the spring of 1997.

"The year before, Amr just shut out everything that hurt him," says Tareq. "It all came back to haunt him, and strongly too. I remember being on the phone with him and Amr just not talking at all. He was so far away from everything. No one knew what he was thinking about."

Amr refused therapy. One of Ben's friends was a psychologist and offered help but Amr completely rejected all forms psychological help. "I will be fine," he would tell people. But he wasn't fine. Amr was not happy with the fast life of New York. He was not happy living without a big house full of people that entertained him. He was not happy having to rely on himself and not being able to call mommy every time something went wrong financially or emotionally. He was just not happy at all.

Then Amr made the biggest mistake of his life. He went home.

One morning in October of 1997, Amr left their apartment early as if he was going to a business meeting. Ben was still sleeping, and remembers getting a kiss and "I love you." When Ben didn't hear from Amr all day that day, and he came back home at night and did not find Amr there, he was worried. He got a frightening call that night from Tareq whom Amr called from Europe on his way home. Ben knew it was the worst news of his life. And what frightened Ben the most was the fact that Amr did not take one item from their home. He did not pack anything. He left most of his credit cards. It was as if Amr did not plan at all to leave and, worse, to ever come back.

Amr had three uncles, and they were all rich and powerful. One of them, the oldest in the family, was a religious man who lived in Medina—Islam's second holiest city. Amr went to him, came out to him and asked for religious help. At loss what to do with his nephew, the uncle called Amr's father. According to Tareq, who got the information from a cousin of Amr who is gay, the father asked for his son to be killed.

"He said to his brother, 'look, if he comes back alive I can tell you right now that I will not be living anymore. This is my only chance. Kill my son.'" Tareq continued to tell me that the uncle pleaded for Amr's life but it was finally agreed that he would hold him there until the father returned from Europe.

Amr was told he was getting some religious help. With a few men from the family, the uncle went into the desert and kept Amr at a site in the middle of nowhere. His father came and his hands eventually beheaded Amr. His body was buried there. And they all returned as if nothing had happened.

The family told everyone that Amr got sick and died in Jeddah. Ben refuses to talk about Amr today. He says that he "would rather remember the sweet soul that came into my life, that loved me beyond I ever imagined someone could love, and treasure that memory in a positive way."

Ben is now single and has been ever since Amr was killed. He is in therapy, trying to get over the loss.

Tareq continues to remember his friend.

"There is not a day that goes by that I don't think about him," he says, with trembling voice of sadness. "I hate what they did to him. He did not deserve to die so young. He was only 36, you know?"

the beiruti hussler

On the north shore of western Beirut, where the city meets the Mediterranean Sea, is an area known as Corniche—miles of waterfront promenade that stretch from the Phoenicia Hotel to Luna Park. With its open-air cafes, breezy palm trees and mesmerizing views, Corniche is perhaps the Beirutis' favorite spot for romance.

"Not everyone is here for romance," says Basil, a 25-year-old man who stands out with his spiked blonde-highlighted hair and huge Dolce & Gabbana sunglasses, worn over a pink tank top. "So many people are here for different reasons. I, for example, am here to make some extra money. Love and romance is waiting at home far from this beach."

Basil is one of the many men here on the Avenue de Paris who indiscriminately sleeps with men and women for a negotiated price. They are usually young and come here for many different reasons. Some are gay teenagers whose parents have kicked them out, while others are heterosexuals coming from disadvantaged backgrounds and whose ways of making a living is through prostitution.

"It is dangerous working here," Basil explains, "first of all, it is illegal to have gay sex, but also prostitution is illegal in this country. Many of the families here are very conservative, Christian and Muslim alike. We risk a lot to be on this street."

Article 534 of the Lebanese Penal Code makes it illegal to have homosexual sex. And whether they are straight or gay, most of these men would not identify as homosexual. Basil, however, identifies as gay and has a boyfriend at home.

"It is stupid to be here if you don't know who you are," he says, with confidence. "Some of the guys here are straight and are doing this for money. I have met some of them over the years who ended up crazy because of not being able to separate their lives from what they do. They make the money but they blame themselves for the way they made the money, especially having to sleep with other men."

He lives in Beit Mery, sixteen miles away from Beirut, with his boyfriend Mikhael. The two of them are enjoying a luxury apartment owned by Mikhael's uncle who lives in Paris. The quiet life in this upscale, and mainly Christian, suburb complements his hectic life in the capital. Being a full time receptionist at a busy dental office during the day, hustling a few nights a week on the Corniche, and tending to the needs of a relationship would stress anyone out.

"I can handle it most of the time," he says, looking left and right as if he is waiting for someone and not sure from which direction they will come. "It is just that sometimes my life gets really busy and I don't have any time for myself. During those times I get lousy, and, of course, my boyfriend often gets the brunt of it."

Many years ago, a friend of his from school named Walid introduced Basil into the hustling business. Walid had already been in the sex industry since he was thirteen and encouraged Basil to try it out. And like many young men on this popular street, Basil felt there was an economic opportunity in selling his body.

"He [Walid] always had extra money, and we wondered where it came from," Basil says of his friend. "And eventually he told me that he was getting it from having sex with people. He didn't know I was gay and so he tried to encourage me by telling me there are women who come to pay handsome men. I was very interested because it was a lot of money."

Walid omitted, however, that most customers would be expatriates—unhappy with their married life or lonely single life—and almost always a lot older. While Basil didn't mind having sex with men, although he says at the time he was not sure if he was bi, or gay, or a confused heterosexual, he was having a hard time going to bed with men often three times his age.

"I could not do it," he says of the older men. "In my family we are taught to respect older generation and I could not imagine having sex with someone that old with or without making money. It seemed very wrong to me. So I would stick with the younger ones."

Overtime, he learned that in such business being picky is not too productive. In a scene heavily used by tired and unhappy middle-aged businessmen far from their home countries, he saw others making more money with the people he was turning down. Not wanting his friend to lose out, Walid began to offer his highest paying clients to Basil.

"One of the clients Walid introduced me was nearly seventy," he says of a retired American man. "I refused at first because he seemed older than my own grandfather, but Walid insisted that John was a great guy. So I gave him a chance, and he became a very good friend and helped me through a lot."

John was a man who retired from the US Navy. When he was a young man he once passed through Lebanon, falling in love with its culture and people. This led to a twice-year visit to the country ever since. A few months after he met the then 19-year-old Basil, he began to visit more and more often. When Basil moved out of his family house because of his sexuality, John rented an apartment for the young man and sometimes would stay for more months.

"Without him, I don't know what I would have done," says Basil of John. "He introduced me to an elegant life. I discovered so much about Beirut that I had never known. He even took me to Paris one summer. He was like a father to me, so we stopped having sex."

Last year, John died of cancer. The tragedy sent Basil into a deep depression. But with Walid on his side, he was able to get past it and come back to the Corniche.

"Walid is so important to me," says Basil, continuing, "I love him more than my own brothers. He is like a business partner, best friend, and life partner all rolled into one."

As the sun is setting over the Mediterranean Sea, Basil and his friend Walid are on the look out for potential customers. Looking at them from afar, you would never think so. They are hanging out with few other guys, all hustlers, and are dancing to a big stereo blasting latest hip-hop songs. Everything looks innocent enough.

"We never really look like we are looking," explains Basil, laughing. "It is so much better if the other people don't know exactly what we are doing. I'm sure some suspect it because we are all here a lot of the time. I really don't care; it is just that it makes the clients feel more confident."

Later, a middle-aged man driving a Mercedes signals to Basil. Without anyone noticing, Basil gets into the car and they drive off. I later find out he is one of Basil's regulars. He is a married man, who divides his time between Paris where his wife and children live and Beirut where he works, and comes to see the young man about once a week.

"He pays really good," says Basil. "I sometimes wonder if he likes me for more than sex. One night he left me with $1000. I didn't work for weeks after that, because that was enough! But after John I decided I don't want to get used to anyone from this business."

A thousand dollars is about 1.5 million Lebanese pounds. Twice a teacher's salary, it is a lot of money for a one night's work. I ask if Basil ever finds young men he wants to date via the business. "No," he insists. "I love my boyfriend, and he is more than enough for me when it comes to love. Even when I meet hot guys, I still remind myself that I'm doing it only for the money."

His boyfriend has no idea that Basil does this for a living. As far as he knows, Basil's only job is as a receptionist at his uncle's dentist office.

"I was doing this before I met him," says Basil. "I really don't feel like he needs to know at this point in our lives. Besides, I only work a few hours here and there. I never do it too long. I work perhaps two or three times a week, and only couple hours each time."

Basil says he has a few rules to protect his relationship with his boyfriend. For example, he swears he never has sex with anyone unless they use condom; they never kiss; he never performs oral sex on them; they are not allowed to penetrate him; and no personal information is exchanged.

"And I never take time from my relationship; if I can't make the money, I go home," he adds. "I only work when my boyfriend either has school or is doing something else, or I want to give him time to be with himself. Some of the clients ask you to stay more than you really have to, and I always turn that down."

As the business of hustling is unpredictable, and not something you can really schedule in a conservative country like Lebanon, where it can lead to years in prison, sometimes Basil goes home with men who are dangerous. He recalls, for example, one night where a woman came home to her husband and Basil having sex on their bed.

"She was so upset, she ran into the kitchen and grabbed a knife," he says. "I was terrified and from that night I decided that I would only go to hotels unless it was someone I already knew is either not married or his wife lives outside of the country like the French man and some others from the Gulf [of Arabia]."

Sometimes he has sex with local men and they don't pay him. This is the reason he now prefers expatriates, he says. On the few nights he gets customers who actually pay, however, he makes a large amount of money in a short amount of time because he has worked very hard to look like what many gay men desire, especially those from the West.

"I lift weights about three times a week," he says, flexing his big biceps, "it gets me noticed out of crowds. Most guys here are slim, not really built. I can ask for a higher price and get it just because of my abs or because I tell them I have a large penis. They go crazy and give me whatever I want. I'm a businessman, so I always ask for a fair price."

Don't let the confident talk fool you. Basil's world is not as cut and dry. He grew up in West Beirut in the 1980s and 1990s with conservative Muslim parents and older brothers who chastised for him for acting girlish. Today, although he is very masculine, he says he still has issues with being feminine. And, although he admits he is gay, he has a hard time with his sexuality and the views he thinks his faith bears on that.

"I don't believe it is okay to be gay," he says in a sad voice, "I think Allah created all of us to be men and have children. I believe I will go to hell if I continue to do this. I still want to change, and sometimes I pray to Allah to change me to normal. I know I can't live like this forever. I have to grow up one day and become responsible for my life like Allah expects us to do."

Even after years in a relationship with another man, whom he says keeps him very happy, Basil does not think gay relationships are healthy or even last.

"I'm different from my brothers because of my gayness," he argues. "If I'm not in a relationship, maybe I will be able to change. I think it is possible. I don't think this life is going to be like this. My boyfriend and I have nothing to connect us like a wife and children would connect with me, you know what I mean?"

Basil comes from an educated, wealthy family: his parents are successful business owners; the oldest brother is a prominent doctor; another is successful lawyer; and one of the sisters holds a high position in the government. Basil talks about how accepting the family is of gay friends and colleagues.

"There is a good friend of my father who everyone knows is homosexual," says Basil. "He has had a partner for many years and both are always invited as a couple to family gatherings. I have never heard of any negative talk about them."

Yet, the family is extremely homophobic towards their son: his father will not talk to him today mainly because of his sexuality, and partly because Basil did not become a doctor or lawyer but art historian; his mother ignores his sexuality; and his siblings are always on his case about seeking help in becoming heterosexual.

When they learned he was in a relationship with Mikhael, a Lebanese Christian, their worst fears about him not changing came true.

The only family who is accepting of him is his uncle, a dentist who gave him a job at his office. However, at work no one knows about his homosexuality because his uncle, however accepting, does not want to alienate any customers. Because he needs the stable income, Basil conforms.

Basil lives in a complicated world full of contradictions and worries. But tonight, that is all for tomorrow to worry about: he comes home, and finds his partner had already cooked dinner and put in the DVD player a new Tom Cruise flick Basil was dying to see. Beaming with happiness, he joins the man he loves in the couch where they cuddle up and agree to watch the film before eating.

familial intifada

In 1949, Sami's family left their home in Jerusalem. Like hundreds of thousands of Palestinians, they became refugees all over the world. Sami's family went to Saudi Arabia where one of the uncles was working.

"I think it was the only country in the world where we knew someone," says Sami. "It was not an easy choice but it was easier than going to Lebanon or Jordan, our neighbor countries but of whom we knew no one."

Sami was only four years old.

In Saudi Arabia, a new kingdom was coming to terms with its own prejudices about its own people when the Palestinian plight first began. And Sami grew up right in the middle of it all.

"I remember being ridiculed as a Palestinian, people calling me all sorts of names in school," he recalls. "I don't remember all the hardships my family remembers from early days in Palestine but I was disgusted with the way I was treated in that country although I was Muslim, Arab and most of all a human being."

Sami says that is one of the main reasons why he chose to move to Jerusalem when he was only seventeen. In Israel, he says, he could at least "understand the racism of the Israelis, it was okay. I can always take the racism and prejudices of someone else but I can never take the racism and prejudices of my own people."

By the age of twenty, Sami discovered the reason why he was never interested in women. He was a homosexual.

"It never occurred to me," he says, laughing. "Perhaps because I never had the chance, I went from an anger to anger. I never could think sexually about those abusive Saudi men. And when I came here, the same became true with the Israelis. I was always a person who believed I wanted to find happiness outside of my own culture and so Palestinians were out of the question, as well." He laughs, and adds, "Just my luck."

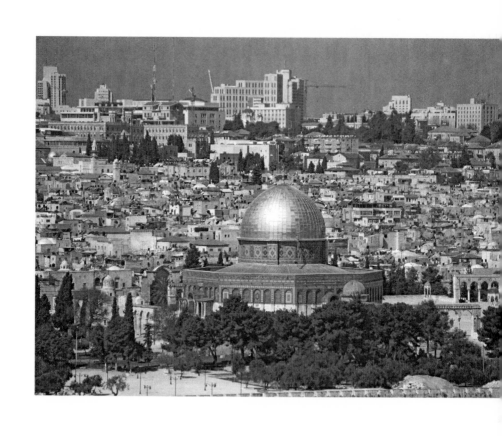

That all changed in a matter of hours one fine morning in 1974. While vacationing in Haifa, with an Arab friend from France, Sami met Spanish-born Jewish activist named Rudolph. He was no ordinary Jew. In fact, Sami never thought he was Jewish.

"He was wearing a shirt with a flag I was not familiar with, which I later found out was the Brazilian flag," remembers Sami. "And to make matters more complicated, he was wearing a beautiful chain with a cross pendent!"

It turned out Rudolph was an activist of, amongst other things, religious pluralism. After a passionate discussion about religion, Sami was sold.

"He shocked people with the truth," says Sami. "And that attracted me more than anything else."

On their second date, Sami found out that Rudolph was Jewish. This was a time when things were still fresh, when generations like Sami and Rudolph still remembered the wars and all that was divisive.

"But Rudi was an exception," says Sami, "because he was a generous person. He was against many of the problems in Palestine. He and I agreed on so many issues."

But some things would have to be ignored. "I just had to forget that he was Jewish," he adds, with a laugh.

The men fell in love so easily. Rudolph was working in Tel Aviv, and unemployed Sami decided to join him there.

"I did not want to live with him," says Sami. "I wanted to find work and support myself but Rudolph was not allowing it. I had to concede."

Sami found work. Soon, he no longer needed to depend on Rudolph. Not financially, at least. They became an equal couple.

"I was young and to have found love and companionship was enough, but to find independence and self-reliance was something even far sweeter."

Tel Aviv, however with a Jewish majority, allowed far more opportunity for Arabs to find work, says Sami.

"Somehow Jerusalem was controlled by religious people of both sides," he remembers, "and that just did not allow the same opportunities. In Tel Aviv you met many Jews who were very secular. Many of them, as I found out, were against Zionist ideologies. This was something I did not know when I was in Jerusalem. We hated Tel Aviv because it was the internationally recognized capital of Israel."

Happy life was interrupted when Sami's family came back to Palestine. They moved to East Jerusalem. And Sami was invited to move back.

"I refused," he says. "Why should I move? I was happy with Rudolph and my life in Tel Aviv."

A cousin from his mother's side was to be given in marriage to Sami. This is why the family wanted him to move there, but Sami was clueless. When he refused outright to move back, they insisted that he at least visit. So he did.

Big mistake.

Unaware to him, the Palestinian boy his family knew became very gay, says Sami. "My hair, my clothes and everything about me was very fashionable," he remembers, laughing. "I was dressing up like John Travolta, and reminded people of Donna Summer because my hair was so big as well as my skin being so dark from spending so much time on the hot beaches of Tel Aviv and Haifa. This gave me away, I guess. I was a complete stranger to them. Not at all someone they remembered. I did not talk, dress or look like them anymore. Everything was different."

After taunting days about marriage and his looks, Sami came out to his family. As a very secular family, he was surprised that they made a big deal about his homosexuality. But he says his relationship with the Jewish man became the biggest obstacle. This was not surprising at all but he never thought it would become bigger than his sexuality.

"They were so upset. 'A Jew? Why?' I was asked," he says. "My mother told me that she could accept a son who became a *manyak* [faggot] but not a son who betrayed his people. The fact that Rudolph was critical of Israel did not matter to any of my family."

In fear of what his family might do, Sami left his family in the middle of one night. By the next morning, he was on his way to Tel Aviv. Rudolph was happy Sami was back safe.

"He was scared they would do something to me," says Sami, "as I were. It was not at all uncommon for people to hurt their loved ones for reasons beyond our understanding of love. My culture, and I think all of Arab culture, is very protective of family honor."

Sami continued to have a dialogue with his family, but he never returned to them again. After a few years, his father died.

"He was upset with me for not marrying," remembers Sami. "I think the older he got, the more he realized he needed children around him. My father spent so many years working for us that he never spent much quality time with us. I think he wanted to have a different relationship with his progeny."

And soon his oldest sister, who had moved to Canada prior to that, took their mother to live with her. Later, the mother would die from brain tumor.

"Mother was so kind," says Sami. "Although she never talked about it, I think she began to accept my sexuality and my relationship with Rudi."

His only brother settled in London, marrying a white Muslim woman.

Sami and Rudolph began a quiet life. Sami studied more Islam and became more religious.

"My [paternal] grandfather was a very religious man, a sheikh known for his outright conservative views in the village," he told me, "my father completely turned his back on grandfather's teachings. Somehow, that love for religion shifted to me."

I wondered what Rudolph thought of all this.

"He was concerned at first," says Sami, "but after he realized it didn't change much of who I'm, he was okay with it."

Rudolph continued to be a secular Jew while he took on more Buddhist teachings.

Today, after more than thirty years of ups and downs, Sami continues to be with Rudolph. They live in a quiet neighborhood in Jerusalem, where Rudi teaches Spanish and Sami writes for Arabic newspaper in London. Sami says he achieved a certain "acceptance and love" from studying Islam more. He says he often meets Muslims who disapprove of his sexuality while they admire his knowledge of Islam. How does he reconcile the two?

"I just live my life," he says. "I live the way I see all humans should live: with love for ourselves and others."

algiers, je t'aime

"'The love of a woman is the likeness of a fine wine that nourishes the soul,' reads an ancient Arabic poem," says Saida, a thirty-something lesbian who lives in Bahrain. "Those who know the poem know it is an anonymously authored one. Deep in my heart, I believe it was a woman who wrote that. No one else can know how a woman can love like that. Whether a mother or a sister or a partner, a woman knows how to love."

Growing up, Saida was influenced by French films. She used to sneak into her parent's bedroom where the television was kept, and watch same films over and over. "Belle de Jour made me who I am today," she says, laughing. "I must have seen it at least a thousand times. You think I'm joking? I watched it almost everyday for years!"

But over all, it is the Arab literature that she finds most intriguing.

"There is just so much deep love," says Saida. "It is often the women, too! I do not think I really believe women love more than men, but only a woman can know how a woman loves. You just can't beat it."

At the age of seventeen, Saida fell in love with another girl, a neighbor. She was an older girl, and already spoken for in marriage although still living at home. Saida knew the risks but she was still overtaken by the feeling.

"I would get a weak feeling in the knees and butterflies in my stomach whenever I saw or spoke to her," she says. "I was shocked by it as I never had—or at least didn't know—any feelings for women. I was terrified of what my family would do to me if they had found out. I read stories in the newspapers about sisters whose brothers found them doing 'immoral' practices with other women. Such sisters ended up dead. Their brothers only serving less than a year in jail time. I did not want to be one of those sisters."

Having four older brothers, Saida knew her actions were carefully watched by all of her family members, as she had reached the age when a woman is given into a marriage. But she was still in love, and didn't know what to do.

"I was very confused," she says, showing the photo of a beautiful woman. "Should I tell her; should I not; would she accept my love; would she report me to the government; would she tell my family; what would she do. I did not know what to do. I decided to keep my mouth shut. It was safe."

Unfortunately for her, Saida was given into a marriage to a man in that same year.

"He was a spoiled brat," she says, throwing her hand in the air. "He was gone, studying abroad—not enough education in my book, as he came back to Arab world to marry a woman in an arranged marriage."

He was twenty-seven, she was seventeen. Ten years difference. He was already sexually experienced, whereas Saida was not.

"I tried to accommodate him," she says, smiling. "I tried two times a week as far as sex goes. He was young and really sexual, each session was longer than the last. I couldn't take that."

It was physically uncomfortable. She did the only thing a teenager would think of. "I faked a sickness," she says, proudly laughing. "I told him that I kept having blood down there. He took me to the hospital and they could not find anything."

Finally, they found a specialist.

"I secretly told the doctor that I was saying I hurt not because I do but because sex was hard for me, as it hurt on an emotional level. The doctor, a woman, decided to tell the husband that we shouldn't have too much sex. This was, of course, against her ethics and I really appreciated it very much."

After being there for a few months, and not much sex, he went back aborad and said he wanted to take another wife.

"I gladly let him do it," says Saida. "This gave me a lot of freedom, as sometimes a whole month would pass without even having sex with him. I never complained about that."

Six years later, Saida met the same woman she was in love with. She had been married with children. This time, however, Saida was older and wiser.

"I expressed to her that I had feelings for her," she says. "She didn't return the love, but promised to keep my secret, saying she felt flattered by my love. I understand now that this was somewhat like a permission to my heart to love other women."

Soon, Saida met a woman named Sihaam through a lesbian gathering in her country. They did not want to have sexual relationship, as they were both married, but became good friends with a lot of hot feelings between them.

"One night, we had sex," she says, smiling. "Then we decided to stay together. It wasn't the best thing to do but we did it anyway!"

Sihaam's husband worked in Algeria where he was having affairs with all sorts of women. This gave the women opportunity to be together. Saida would join Sihaam in Algiers, lying to her family.

"I would pretend to go helping out 'my' friend because, of course, she was sick and all," says Saida. "In reality, we were together while he went about with his affairs."

A few years afterwards, each of the women divorced. They opened their own business in Algiers, where they began a life together.

"Living with a woman I love has taught me happiness," she says. "We raise our children in the best manner possible. We teach them love and tolerance. We give them the peace of mind of having two mothers. And they feel special that, unlike most of their friends, they have two mothers who are at home together most of the time."

But it is not always easy. Saida says it is not easy being a lesbian in an Arab society, let alone raise children or have a proper home.

"The hardest thing is that we have to ask the children to lie," she says, "which is something we really hate to do to them. We wish we didn't have to ask them to keep our relationship a secret. But I would rather have them lie than being taken away from their parents or, even worse, know their parents are killed because of their sexuality."

With so much to risk, love seems to bring them a peace of mind.

the cairene diaries

Smoking one session of *sheesha*—which can last for hours—might be the equivalent of 18 cigarettes, but it is not a problem for Galal. Confidently, he inhales the tobacco outside the popular El-Fishawy café in Cairo's Khan El Khaleely neighborhood.

"You only die once," reasons Galal, a 27-year-old gay man who lives miles away from the chaos here. "I can be killed by anything. Why worry about the risks of life's enjoyments? Sheesha is my favorite pastime. Even when I was a child, I loved the way it felt to be around it. It is magical!"

In the crowded alleys of old Cairo, Egyptians walk carelessly in neighborhoods many Westerners would think of as dangerous. And this is specially the case when you are young and gay in the heart of Islamic Cairo, where even if you escape the secular national laws you are still faced with religious ones—sometimes far more damning the state's colonial rules. But in a city like Cairo, taking risks are only part of the everyday life.

"I could be arrested or killed any moment," explains Galal, who says most people suspect he is gay because of his feminine demeanor. "But what will worrying about that solve for me? Nothing. I'm enjoying my life. I will deal with the stones life throws at me," he adds.

Galal has been arrested many times before.

The first time he went to jail, it was on charges of obscene behavior. It happened in Alexandria where he was born and raised. He was then a 21-year-old prostitute, working with the locals and foreigners alike. And one night, one of his customers proposed that they have sex in public. "He was very sexy, and talked to me in a way no one has ever done before. It was the customer from heaven. I couldn't resist his orders," remembers Galal.

That "customer" ended up being a secret policeman.

"I was in jail that time for four days," recalls Galal. "I had no experience with being in jail. I was young and naïve. They beat me so frequently that I

went home with four broken ribs. What I don't forget until this day is the way it smelled. No one washed the floors. And it was clear there had been a lot of urinating going on. Aargh!"

The second time he was arrested, it was three years later when he first came to Cairo. He fought with another young man who made homophobic jokes about him. He snapped and broke the guy's nose. He was in jail for nearly a month. Immediately after he got to jail, one of the guards began to sexually abuse him.

"I wouldn't have minded if they fucked me all they wanted, because I would pay any policeman to fuck me," he says, laughing, "but they hurt me with [policeman] sticks, tearing my insides. There is nothing pleasurable about that."

Another time, Galal met a man on the internet. After they chatted for a long time, they exchanged some nude pictures and decided to go ahead and meet face to face. The man was supposed to be a businessman visiting from Lebanon. Instead, it turned out he was a policeman.

He was raped repeatedly.

"But they were so hot that I really enjoyed half of it!" Galal jokes, adding "'I told them from the first day, 'Do not beat me but do that however long you wish'"—making a circle out of his thumb and index finger on one hand, and inserting his other index finger into the circle; indicating sexual intercourse.

Galal might crack jokes about the horrible things that have happened to him in order to appear tough, but underneath it all he has a heart as soft as he speaks. Even though his parents rejected him because of his perceived sexual weakness, he continues to send money home month after month. He works up to sixteen hours on certain days in order to make enough to send back. Sometimes he sends $200 a month, other months he sends as much as $500—depending on what is going on.

"If there is a wedding," he says, showing me a picture of his sister getting married, "I have to then send more, of course. When my sister got married, I threw her a wonderful wedding because the man she married was a young guy who didn't have any money."

But it is not just weddings.

"When my mother's young brother died, I had to send a lot more back because the man left a wife and children. I don't feel so bad about it because he really helped my mother when I was growing up. So it was a way for me to pay him back."

To make sure he makes enough money, on certain occasions, Galal has gone back to his old life; he will sleep with men for money. He is now far pickier than his old days. Usually, it is wealthy men from Cairo's high society who get him in bed.

"But even then I still feel a bit dirty," he says, in a confessional kind of way. "It is not what I would like to do, but the money is really good. It is not a job. I'm not one of those people who can say, 'Oh, it is just work' and are able to separate from their conscious. No, it is not because I feel dirty every time I do it."

I ask if it is worth to risk his safety. After all, if he was entrapped before by one of his clients what makes him think another one can't do the same?

"Honey," he says, laughing, "I can tell you with certainty that these men have far more to lose than I. Some of them are in high places in politics, or have power. Some are celebrities that have to keep up a certain reputation. I have diaries and diaries, and they all know. I could destroy their lives. So don't worry about me!"

a few good women in cairo

More than sixty years ago, a little girl by the name of Farduz found herself "lusting after women," as a friend of hers puts it. That wasn't just unacceptable but also unheard of in her community—a small village right in the middle of Egypt.

Farduz grew up to become a beautiful woman, married a man and later reconnected with her sexual desire to women.

"She was what I call fierce fem," says Sharifa Ismail, an Iraqi-born lesbian who worked with Farduz for more than twenty years. "She was everything we wanted to be: beautiful, gentle, feminine and fierce!"

In 1963, while she was married, one night Farduz set up a "gathering" for the lesbians in her country. That night, for the first time in their lives, those Arab women had the privilege to be in the company of other lesbians and not feel ashamed or scared.

Of course, with a good thing like that, they had to repeat it. And repeat it. And repeat it. It became a monthly meeting and used to just be called "the gathering" and one year after their first meeting, the women decided to make it more "official." They wanted a name, and so they called it *Hamd*, a word that means "to praise."

"It was 1979, if I remember it correctly, when I was introduced to them by a friend," says Sharifa, who lived in Iraq at the time. "Maybe it was a long commute, but it was worth it. I would go there for the big meetings that happened every six months."

In 1987, after coordinating the meetings for more than twenty years, Farduz died from pneumonia. As can be imagined, the women felt lost without her.

"It was devastating day for all of us," says Sharifa. "To this day, we still mourn her every year. She was young. She should have lived to be hundred!"

After Farduz died, her best friend, also a lesbian and a member of the group, took over.

"It wasn't easy," says Istaqlal, the current coordinator of Hamd. "I was the oldest of us, so that is why the women chose me. No one has the talent she had. She was the kind of person who put smile on your face by just watching her face. She always was happy. In our hearts, no one can take her place."

Hamd is very closeted and does not have any public meetings where anyone can come. The meetings almost always happen between their homes. For example, Fatma, a woman in Alexandria, hosted the last three months. The fifty-two women who are members all know and trust each other, says Istaqlal. Whenever a new member comes, it is because one of them trusts that person.

In fact, Hamd is so closeted that a gay Arab activist, Abu Omar, who lives in Cairo, did not know about them. Abu Omar, who has lesbian friends himself, only got in touch with the group after he was invited to write a story about them for *Huriyah*. He said he didn't believe it until he saw a house full of "strong, butch women," though Istaqlal says the group is "very mixed" in terms of feminine vs. butch.

Their finance is also another interesting story. At every meeting, the women bring whatever they can and donate it to the woman who hosts the next meeting.

"It is not intimidating, so it works for us," says Istaqlal, who mostly hosts it at her houses in Cairo and Asyut, where she is originally from and owns a farmhouse. "We put the [donation] box in the back and nobody sees what you put in it. You put in whatever you can."

Also, they receive small monies from abroad. For example, members like Sharifa (who lives in Canada) and Marium (in Germany) support them. In 2003, for example, Sharifa, Marium and Suleika (another member in the UK) put together $2,500. That allowed the women to rent an entire boat in the Nile River and party like it is nobody's business in celebration of their 40th anniversary.

"We enjoyed it much," says Istaqlal, who pulled off planning the party with a few other women. "It was like a wedding. We are thankful to our sisters for coming and supporting us like that."

Hamd is not just a partying club, however. In 2001, when two women from their group were arrested in mass with many other queer people on a boat now mostly known as "Cairo 52"), Istaqlal and her assistant went down to the police station in Cairo with two men, whom they paid to say they were married to the women. They were let go.

In 2002, when a member had to have a complicated surgery, Hamd members pulled together and paid for her to have a first-class surgery in Dubai, UAE.

"It felt good to do that for our sister," says Istaqlal. "We are blessed to have each other like this."

But Hamd's work goes beyond Egypt. When in 1994 a member moved to neighboring Libya, she started a group of her own, which she also named Hamd. That group now has over twenty strong members in Tripoli, the capital. Hamd Egypt supports them almost exclusively.

"The success of their story is their secrecy," says Abu Omar, speaking about the women. "They are very smart women. No one suspects them. I support them being secretive because their lives are at stake. The society here would accept a gay man much faster than it would accept a lesbian. Their lives would be threatened. If not by the government, by their families."

Istaqlal says whenever they rent a place—which is not often—they tell the people it is for a wedding.

"It is easier this way," says Istaqlal, who plans another big party later that year to welcome the Islamic holy month, Ramadan. "Arab people are nosey. You must tell them something. We are curious people, you see, in our nature. It is easy for us to not be noticed because we don't do public events. No parade. Just in our homes we celebrate."

ashnas and mehboobs: an afghan love story

When the Taliban was ousted from Afghanistan, the media was filled with stories about Afghans returning to cinema halls, flying kites, and playing music. And yes, to an Afghanistan where older men were once more openly courting teenaged boys.

As a queer Muslim living in the West, I was concerned. Here we go, I thought, more bad press for queer people. Now we were back to stereotypes of child molesters. But I knew from my own background that the story is not simply about pedophilia—culture and tradition are all woven into it. So I decided to get the story directly from the source.

This is where Sadar comes in. He is a 28-year-old Afghani man who now lives in Pakistan. He doesn't want his last or family name revealed. A transsexual Pakistani friend of mine found him for me.

Until he moved to Pakistan at the age of 19, Sadar was an *ashna*. The word means "beloved" but has the context of "boy toy" in Afghani culture. When he was 14, an older man, who was 35 at the time, from a village near his bought him a cup of tea one day. Sadar was in the teashop and, since it is part of their culture to be hospital, which includes but is not limited to buying tea for others, he was not alarmed by it. The two talked and the older guy asked Sadar if he would meet him for tea the next day. Sadar says the older man kept making tea appointments for the two of them for about a fortnight. Then, one day the older man arrived at the teashop with a gift, an expensive shawl from either Pakistan or India.

"I was surprised," says Sadar. "It was a pretty shawl. I wasn't interested in it, though. I didn't like masculine things and that shawl was masculine." Sadar remembers being different as a boy. He didn't "fancy" all the stuff the other boys liked. "I was apart from the boys," he says. "I liked feminine things. So I took the shawl and gave it to my father. I told him I bought it for him."

After accepting that gift, Sadar felt obligated to continue meeting the man. They now started taking walks together and slowly become close. Sadar found a lot that he liked in the man. "He was tender," he says. "He would ask me if needed water or anything all the time. He was protective of me and encouraged me to study. He had been a second father to me. Better father than my own because he didn't judge me."

Sadar says that ever since he could remember his own father made fun of him for being feminine. "He would always say something like 'Why can't you be like your brothers?' and that always hurt because I didn't have an answer for it."

Sadar's friend owned a shop in Sadar's village. One evening, two years after they first met, he invited Sadar to come to the shop and share a dinner with him. Sadar was not surprised when his friend approached him sexually. "I didn't expect that when I went there that night," he says. "I was in love with him by this time, you see."

He says he fell deeply in love with the older man because "he loved me and kept me close." When asked whether their relationship was remotely sexual for those first two years, Sadar says "No. I did have sexual feelings towards him but nothing happened. I suspect he desired me as much but never showed it." And so the older man became Sadar's *mehboob* (lover).

The older man continued to give gifts to Sadar and the couple kept having sex for the next three years. He says everyone was aware of their relationship and no one questioned them about it. "People figured it out before I did," he says, laughing. "You just don't talk about those sorts of things, though, so I didn't know." He says he felt it was something that was happening only to him.

But he knows now that was not true. Afghani culture has been replete with similar stories for thousands of years. At the end of his translation of *1001 Arabian Nights*, the 19th century British explorer Richard Burton wrote: "The Afghans are commercial travelers on a large scale and each caravan is accompanied by a number of boys and lads almost in woman's attire with kohl'd eyes and rouged cheeks, long tresses and henna'd figners and toes, riding luxuriously in *kajawas* or camel panniers: they are called *kuch-i safari*, or traveling wives, and the husbands trudge patiently by their sides."

Sadar confesses that he did put on women's stuff occasionally when he was having sex or sometimes when he was just around his older friend. "I only did that because it made the relationship more pure," he says, adding that having sex when dressed as a woman somehow made it less "evil," because even though the culture allows it, Afghani Muslims consider sexual relationship between two males a gross sin. "I wore *surma* [a dark toxic eye liner] and painted my lips. Then I'd put on a feminine shawl. It pleased him. He would get excited even more!"

At this point, I ask Sadar whether his "friend" was single or not. "He was married," he says. "He had a wife and three children. He was devoted to his family." Then I ask him whether he ever entertained the idea of the two of them settling down together. "Well, that doesn't exist in our culture," he says. "I was really happy to see him three or four times a week." For the last three years of the relationship (from Sadar's age of 16-19) they were having sex three to four times a week! At that point, I wondered whether the older man abandoned his wife in bed. "No, we would have sex early in the evening or early in the morning," says Sadar. "And he would go to bed with his wife at night. This man was strong enough to do it more than several times, I think."

For most Afghanis, the relationship between the ashna and mehboob was very acceptable, says Sadar. For example, one of the most famous poems (also a marching song) called *Zakhmi Dil* or "Wounded Heart" has a very homoerotic ending: "There is a boy across the river with a bottom like peach, but alas I cannot swim." The poem conveys the impression that one can lust after boys and be macho at the same time, which is what most Afghanis expect. There are hundreds of more poems like the above, where poets talk about love for boys.

However a gay relationship in western sense is impossible to imagine in Afghanistan, let alone accept. "What would be of the use?" When I ask whether Afghanis could ever accept two men being in a relationship or even getting married to each other, Ghedar Ahmed, an Afghan-American in San Francisco, asks. "Why would anyone want to have a relationship like that with another man?" And Ahmed is not even an immigrant—he is an Afghan-American born and raised in San Francisco, America's most famous "gay Mecca." So it is not surprise to hear what a Pathan in midland Afghanistan would say.

Mahmoud Esmayel is from Kabul, Afghanistan's capital. He says "[a ga relationship] is western evil thought that is harmful to human race." Then explain to him that in the West, we not only have older men who fancy younge men but that some even get married to each other to profess their love for one another. "Love?" Esmayel asks. "What is there to be loved? It is lust. They lust after each other and the husband goes home to his wife. We accept that."

I ask Sadar whether the older man ever told him he loved him. "Oh, yes," he says. "Every time we met or parted, he would kiss my eyes and lips and tell me he loved me." And when asked whether he said the same back, he says yes. I say I find it hard to understand how a man can tell you he loves you and you tell him you love him and at the same time have no thoughts for a future together. "The idea just doesn't come to you," says Sadar. "All these permanent relationship for men is western. They are nice ideas but impossible in Afghanistan."

So what happened to their relationship? "Afghanistan became a country too hard to live in," says Sadar. "War and so much destruction. I always wanted to come to Pakistan and my mehboob found me enough money for me to come here." Do they keep in touch? "No. He once sent a word with someone but that was it." Sadar says he doesn't think his friend found another boy after him mainly because it was very hard to find anyone under the Taliban, who came to power a year before he left. The Taliban were known to put people to death if they were suspected of homosexuality.

I asked Sadar what he himself identified as. He says he identified as a "bedegh [a male passive partner.]" When I ask him if he wants to get married (because nearly all the reports said the ashna goes on to get married) Sadar says he has "no intention of doing so, because I like men too much and like to spend nights of love-making with them. A marriage would make that impossible for me."

Even after nine years, Sadar still has a soft spot for his mehboob and says he will never forget him. No one had even come close to his love, he says. I guess it is true what they about first love.

punjabi melodies

When she was only six years old, Mumtaz was slapped by her grandmother so hard that her loose left cuspid tooth, a fact she had been hiding from family, had fell down. What was her crime? She was caught wearing grandma's panties.

The problem is that Mumtaz was not a girl then. She was a little boy of the same name (the name Mumtaz can be for both genders in South Asian countries). And, in 1960s conservative Pakistan, a little boy wearing his grandmother's underwear is a crime of societal norms that a slap on the cheek would be considered not punishment at all.

"I grew up in a Punjabi working family in 1960s Islamabad," says Mumtaz, now in her late 40s. "The city was then still being built by [president] Ayub Khan, but my family lived in the area for a very long time. My family is very traditional, and this was particularly the case in those days."

In the 1960s, the Pakistani government was building a new capital—far from the sea, where the older capital, Karachi, was vulnerable to an attack by India—near Rawalpindi, a city in the Pothohar Plateau, which was home to perhaps one of the oldest human culture in Asia—the Soan Culture. The Punjabis occupy the whole region of Punjab, which stretches from northwestern India to eastern Pakistan. And even today, they remain a strong majority at nearly 70% in Islamabad.

Mumtaz's father was one of the many government employees who settled in the city, and her mother passed away while giving birth to a son three years younger than Mumtaz. The father took his young orphaned "sons" to his mother, who promised to raise her with love.

"And she did," says Mumtaz, of the woman. "My grandmother taught me a lot. She was often harsh with punishment, but the guidelines she set for me as a child still continue to sanely guide me through life. I don't remember my mother, but I'm a better mother today because of the lessons I learned from my grandmother."

Growing up, life was never easy. Her father fell ill when she was only 14 forcing the young transsexual girl to start working—leaving school behind She kept a little shop in the main market, and was immersed in business tha she no longer had time to go to school as she was struggling to pay for he brother's education.

"I had always felt like a girl," Mumtaz recalls, during that time, "but I had neve really thought about what that meant. I remember being 16 and not wanting girls Like everyone in that situation, I began to think maybe I was homosexual."

As a boy, she was short, petite and feminine. The men would hit on he because she had a beautiful, beardless face. And she fell in love with one of them whose shop was right across from hers. It would prove to be a relationship that would send the confused 17-year-old into journey of self-discovery.

"He was kind to me," she remembers. "His name was Upjeet. He was in his 30s, married, and had children. And it wasn't as if I thought I would marry him or anything like that. The relationship was strictly sexual. I was a boy, after all But I loved him because he loved me. After we were together for months, he began to ask me about my sexuality and gender. When I told him everything I felt about myself, he convinced me that I was a woman and that I only needed the appropriate surgeries to make me complete. It was really amazing."

Soon, everything fell apart. Mumtaz recalls Upjeet complaining about a lower back pain for a few months, and it got worsened overtime. All of a sudden, the man fell really ill and was taken to Campbellpur (Attock) where his family lived—about 50 miles from Islamabad. Mumtaz was heartbroken when she learned he had passed away.

"The news left me empty," she remembers. "I stopped doing everything. I left for Bombay, where a friend of mine invited me to go along. And I stayed there for years because I had nothing left in Islamabad without Upjeet."

After almost ten years, she came back to Islamabad for her grandmother's funeral. Much to her family's shock, Mumtaz was now dressed in *sari* and was looking more beautiful than any other woman at that funeral.

"And to make matters even more complicated, I showed up with a child," she remembers, laughing. "I didn't plan any of it. I had my son, whom I had through one stupid night of passionate lovemaking with a female friend, and I had no one to leave him with in India. I had to bring him along. And I was lready dressing as a female for years before, and had no idea how to go back o male clothing."

What was shocking to Mumtaz is the way her family responded. Everyone greeted her with respect, and no one seemed to care she was now a woman. She left Islamabad to go back to India, with a lot of requests of correspondence with relatives. She did keep one thing secret: that she was a prostitute in India, and that was how she was able to send money back home.

"In India, I didn't care about anything," says Mumtaz. "No one knew me as Mumtaz, the boy from Islamabad. Everyone knew me as Mumtaz, the woman who charmed men out of their pockets. But to me, prostitution was a serious business. If a man was unhappy in his daily life, I could offer him some sort of happiness for however short before he goes to sleep." And then she adds, "I felt it was a good paying job also!"

But in India, Mumtaz also created a circle of good friends—most of them gay or transsexual—and led an enriched life full of love. One of her clients ended up becoming a regular, leading to a yet another love affair with a married man. And although all that was happening, when her father asked her to come back after twenty some odd years to take over the business he had been creating with the money she had been sending, she went back.

"It was good to come back," she says, "I didn't realize how much I missed the people here. They are still good people, untouched by modernization and everything that breaks communities."

But life in Pakistan is not the same as that in India. Whereas her life in India was hectic, her life in Pakistan is quiet. Being an artistic soul, she knew she had to do something to connect with herself. She started doing performances.

"I'm a dancer," she says, "I love to dance. So I started dancing to old Bollywood songs at weddings and birthdays or anyone else who will have me. I will dance anywhere!"

It is a way to balance. Nevertheless, she has no regrets to come back.

"I came back to make my father happy," Mumtaz says. "My brother has gotten married and moved away to Karachi a long time ago. My father is old now. I'm at least able to be here, and provide some sort of family connection for him. And my son is growing up with a decent man in his life. What more could I ask for?"

healings in jakarta

More than eighteen thousand islands make up the Republic of Indonesia. In these tropical islands, there are over two hundred million Muslims—making the country the most populous Muslim-majority nation in the world.

Here, there are over seven hundred ethnic groups, and Gamelan belongs to the largest ethnic group—the Javanese. She was born, raised and lives in Jakarta, the largest city of the island of Java, which also happens to be the capital of the country. "Actually, with about ten million people, Jakarta is more like an international capital," jokes Gamelan, a 36-year-old lesbian marketing executive. "It is a crazy city that keeps us all moving. Not a day goes by that you don't physically bump into someone. Only in Jakarta."

Growing up in a highly liberal Muslim family had its perks for Gamelan. She has lived most of her life with openness and honesty, amongst educated family and friends. For example, at the young age of nine, she told her mother that she wanted to marry a girl and not a boy. A very early indication of her daughter's same-sex feelings, the mother encouraged Gamelan.

"My mother was very compassionate woman to everyone she came across," remembers Gamelan, "I was not surprised the way she accepted me. Since then I have never looked back. Once a girl has her mother's blessing, no one else can bring you down. All of my friends, important relatives and co-workers know. Pretty much everybody knows."

On the corner of the crowded Mangga Bessar and Hayam Wuruk streets, after a busy day at work, Gamelan meets two of her closest friends on a hip bar called New Moonlight. All professional single women in their late twenties, they sit and share their day.

"We really just dream about living in Paris or New York and having a fabulous time," says Gamelan, laughing. "Men always think we are talking about them, which couldn't be further from the truth. We usually talk about our dream jobs. I want to be a fashion designer. Sofia would love to quit her

rchitect job and instead make furniture. Kartini likes being an editor but she vants to own her publishing company, polluting the world with tons of chick ummer reads."

About five years earlier, Gamelan went through a bad break-up. After being n a relationship for more than ten years, Gamelan's Japenese partner left her or another woman and moved back to Tokyo to run a new business with the 1ew woman. Gamelan was devastated.

"It is not the sort of thing you expect," says Gamelan. "It was a blow to ny life. I could not do anything for a year. I was miserable. I felt unwanted ind my self-esteem was below zero. This was someone I planned my whole ife around. I met her when I was twenty. I never for one second thought we vould part alive."

Still in therapy to this day, Gamelan finds herself unable to commit.

"Every time I get to that point with a woman I'm dating, I always pull out," :hares Gamelan, reluctantly. "It is not something I'm proud of. After all, you vould think someone would get over a break up after five years, right? I wish I :ould. I want to be with someone. No one really wants to be alone. And I hate hat I can't allow others into my heart anymore. It is not a fun situation."

It is a good thing she has friends who understand and empathize with her :ituation. Sofia, one of the friends friends, got divorced six years ago from her 1usband. She left the marriage feeling blameful because the husband turned)ut to be homosexual. And even though he told her he was that way before hey got married, she felt responsible for not "turning" him straight.

Katrini's world was compromised when her favorite teacher raped her one ifternoon after school in his home. Although she is not a lesbian, Katrini finds 1ard to trust men and has never developed a long-term relationship with them.

"We are support to each other," says Gamelan, of her friends. "It is always 1s against the world. We would have lived together had it not been that we are ıll so independent and professional."

Heading the marketing department of a large corporation, Gamelan devotes most of her time to making that company's image unforgettable in the minds)f Indonesians. Still, she finds time to have those things that matter to her the most. And, because she continues to defy all stereotypes of what a Muslim woman in her country should be like, I wouldn't worry about her much.

confessions in lahore

Lahore is perhaps the cultural capital of the Muslim nation of Pakistan. As the second largest city in one of the most complicated states of the world, Lahore has had its own turbulent past. According to legends the city was found by Lava, the son of the Hindu God Rama, whose name it bears. Since then, it has changed hands with the empires of the Brahaman, Ghaznavid, Mughal, Sikh and British.

But modern Lahore is a city that best illustrates the diversity of Pakistan—where the leaders might be allies of America's War on Terror but whose tribal-ruled lands might be harboring America's deadliest enemies such as Usama Ben Laden. It is a city where Lollyhood, the country's secular film industry, and some of the largest *madrassas*, religious schools which many say teach extremism, are based.

Thursdays are days looked forward to in Pakistan as they welcome the Muslim weekend. For Nadeem, a successful IT Sales Exec for a software firm, his particular Thursday is one of importance. He is in a hurry but tries to finish markings into his computer after a long day of encouraging representatives from many corporations to make use of his company's latest software before he leaves.

"I'm actually almost late," says Nadeem, as he glances over the clock on the wall. "I should already be on my way, because I'm going to across town. And you know the traffic will not be pleasant."

Nadeem is headed to Samanabad, a middle class residential district, where he will join dozens of other men at the house of one of them. The topics of their conversations will include how to best reconcile their sexuality and their faiths, culture and environment. They are all queer, almost all married with children, and are leading lives they are not exactly happy with.

"We meet there every last Thursday of each month," explains Nadeem, a 39-year-old who happens to be one of the many married fathers. "I wish we could do it more often but most of us are leading busy lives. Some of us don't even make it to every month," he adds.

When he arrives fifteen minutes late to the meeting, he quietly sits in the back. There is a man standing up, speaking in Urdu and talking passionately about his life in the past month. He talks about how he feels horrible that he is hiding his sexuality from his wife, family and people he works with. "It is such a burden," says the man once, in English, emotionally. "When are we ever going to be able to stop letting other people make us feel bad about who we are?"

Later, it is Nadeem's turn. He stand up, apologizes for being late and tells them that he had a long day and to forgive him if he doesn't speak as well as the man before him. "But I'm happy to be here," he says, looking around, "I'm very happy, indeed. I had been looking forward to this meeting, well, since we last saw each other. I have had an easy month… "

Nadeem tells the group that his wife, who is due to give birth in less than a month to their third child, had gone to Karachi to visit her mother and to give birth there. Although he complains about taking care of their old son by taking him to and from school, and hanging out with him a lot, Nadeem says he feels a sense of relief that the wife is gone.

"I know many of you have experienced this, but it feels like I'm lying less," he adds, acquiring nods from many in the group. "But it is still very difficult. I wish, like many of you, I could tell my family and still be accepted."

Nadeem talks about his male lover from work; how he is scared that the man will do something silly at work, and that people at work will find out about Nadeem's sexuality. Although Nadeem spends many nights at the man's house when Nadeem's wife is home, the lover had already kissed him in the lunchroom once at work, though there were not people around. "There could have been someone watching," he says. "I like my job, and I really like this man, but I don't know what to do because I can't risk losing my job."

One by one, the men share what has been going on in their lives since their last meeting. One man talks about coming out to his American friend at the US Consulate in Lahore, and how the man encouraged him not to tell others in fear that he might be assaulted. Another man shares his experience with a taxi driver and how they made love with on the grounds of the Punjab

University—the oldest university in the country. And then there is a young man, whom I later find out is only 19, who details a recent rape by his older cousin. The young man's boyfriend, who brought him to the meeting, later says he had paid for the gang beating of that cousin, who ended up in the hospital.

For almost ten years, Nadeem had been coming to these meetings. Some of the original members, who go back all the way to the 1980s, are still there. Otherwise, members come and members leave once they leave the area or the country. However, there are a few members who come from as far as Islamabad and Karachi, both about 700 miles away.

"I'm not surprised that they come from that far," says Nadeem, who lives in a district not far away from there. "These meetings save our lives," he adds, continuing to say, "I would have suffered mental illness by now if I had not been part of this amazing group of men."

A few years earlier, Nadeem was stationed in Dubai by his company. He missed about a year's worth of meetings then and the man was devastated. "I did not realize how important they were to me," he says of the men most of whom are personal friends now, "I asked to be transferred back in less than 3 months after I left. I could not do it. I mean, there are a large number of gay South Asians in the UAE, but it is just not the same thing."

surabayan secrets

As far as he can remember, the short and small-bodied Hassan has been struggling to explain to others that he is actually a he.

"My first recollection is at age four," says Hassan, who was born and raised in Jakarta, Indonesia. "My mother, who was a very religious woman, beat me after I took my dress off and put pants on. 'You are a girl! Keep your dress on!'"

For 18 years, Hassan was forced to be Rihia. His mother painted his hands, and did everything she could to convince herself and her community that Rihia was just as feminine as any other girl.

"I had to wear the best dresses," remembers Hassan. "My mother spent so much money on this and I hated every minute of it."

That was then. This is now. Hassan now wears whatever he pleases; most days, jeans and T-shirts seem to get lucky.

"It is all about my comfort level," he says, laughing. "I love jeans. And T-shirts are the best things ever invented."

Thirteen years ago, Hassan went to Canada as a student.

"I found a whole new world in Canada," says the now 31-year-old with a little laughter to hide his painful past. "A new system. A system where I could be anyone I wanted to be. Naturally, I overstayed my welcome by a few years."

For years, he dressed as a man and took hormones to be convincing. Naturally, he began to see in the mirror more and more the person he believed he was.

"It was a very interesting process. Within days I knew things were changing in my body, which is a bit unusual. And within months, I was beginning to feel comfortable with my body as I was becoming more masculine, seeing the person I am," he remembers.

Within a year, he was able to ditch "Rihia."

"The trouble was that the more I did the hormones, the more my voice changed, as well," he says, laughing. "So I told my family it was expensive to call and I would just write letters. I wrote many, many letters so that the wouldn't miss the phone calls."

At school, "Rihia" was supposed to have studied Political Science.

"My mother was probably hoping for me to become the next Indonesia female president," says Hassan, laughing at how off base his mother was. "Bu I wanted to become a mechanic because my dream was always to own an aut shop."

Two years later when he went back to Indonesia for a surprise summe visit, Hassan shocked his entire family. No one recognized him. He was a full bearded man. And to make matters worse, he came home with a degree in aut mechanics. As he expected, the family did not like any of it.

"I was pretty much told I could no longer consider myself part of the family," Hassan remembers. "It was one thing to think I would be disowned but it was completely different to be living it. I felt so alone."

It was a price he was willing to pay.

"I packed my bags and came to Surabaya [a city on another island]," he says. "I opened my shop within months, with money I brought with me from Canada and some which I borrowed from old friends. No one knows who am here. As far as anyone knows, I'm just Hassan."

Hassan is not able to change his name or gender status on any of his legal identifications. However, in the business he is in, "no one cares abou identifications anyway," he says. "People are happy with my work. I love wha I do, and it shows in my work. So I have a satisfied clientele."

For now, he lives one day at a time.

"I can't go back," he says, "Hassan is here to stay."

gold in the bay of bengal

As a young bisexual woman in Bangladesh, Farheen was not sure about her arranged marriage. She was only fourteen years old when her family decided she would marry a far cousin named Zayed.

"I knew I was attracted to him," remembers 39-year-old Farheen. "I just didn't know about a marriage where I wasn't allowed to be with women. When you are young, you assume all kinds of things."

Prior to her marriage, Farheen "fooled around with other girls but never with the boys. Boys were reserved for marriage." This was something that continued until she got married.

"A few days before our wedding day," she says, laughing, "I slept with one of his female friends. She was so sexy!"

On their wedding night, Zayed, who is now 42, was both shocked and delighted when his new bride came out to him. "She leaned over and said point blank that she was bisexual," remembers Zayed, who was only seventeen then. "She told me that she liked women as much as she liked men. She seemed to expect some harsh response. I was speechless."

Fearing he might out her, Farheen tried to back out of the conversation realizing what she had just done. "It was just too much bottled inside me," she now recalls, "so I think it came out before I was ready."

Then something happened that she had never expected. Her new husband looked her in the eye and told her that he was bisexual himself. They both started laughing.

"It was not something I was prepared for at all," remembers Farheen. "I do remember feeling like a weight had been lifted off me."

Though both sides of the family prepared the couple for the first night, Farheen and Zayed didn't make love that night. Instead, they spent the entire night sharing and exchanging their sexual fantasies, their difficulties with accepting who they are sexually, et cetera.

"We were both crying and laughing the whole night," says Farheen. "It was he most beautiful night in my life. It was as if my life was just beginning."

Next, the couple asked each what to do.

"Now what?" was what came to them, says Zayed. "It was clear to both of us that we just became the luckiest couple in the world. But we also knew this vas not acceptable in our families."

They agreed that they would try to make their relationship work without leeping with other people.

"That worked great for about six months," says Farheen, laughing. "Then I vanted to bite some breasts!"

And, apparently, she wasn't the only one wanting something else. Zayed confessed that he too wanted to sleep with men. So, naturally, they agreed o try out a kind of relationship where they would be able to see members of same sex while still married. The arrangement would work perfectly—but low? Open relationship was the only way.

Only months after the new relationship was put into motion, the couple ound it hard to keep up their arrangement. They were getting attached to other people. What they decided next would be unacceptable to many people.

"We decided we would find another bi couple and have a foursome relationship," says Zayed. "But they would have to be Muslim. Farheen refused non-Muslims."

Some things are harder to find. Farheen and Zayed never found their Muslim lovers but instead went to a party one night and met a nice spiritual out otherwise non-religious Catholic couple. Far from what they wanted, but hey were nice enough that they felt it was okay.

"Jane was so beautiful," remembers Farheen. "I didn't care if she was not Muslim."

Less than six months after they first met, Farheen and Zayed moved in ogether with Jane and Blake in a two-bedroom house outside of Toronto. The arrangement is now that two sleep together in one room. Never do all four sleep together in one room.

"It simplifies emotions between all of us," says Farheen.

This means once every three days, Farheen and Zayed will sleep together. The rest of the three nights, Farheen sleeps one night with Blake and one night with Jane, and the same for all of them.

Although they are not religious, Farheen and Zayed had to do some house rules with their partners. One of the requests was that Jane and Blake not buy pork or alcoholic beverages.

"But we are very lenient just about everything else," says Zayed.

Blake and Jane, wanting to get to know the culture of their partners, decided they would want to spend time in Bangladesh. Now, thanks to Zayed's good income (his father left him millions of dollars where Zayed bought companies in Bangladesh), they all spend about 6 months a year in Bangladesh. They bought a nice little house by the Bay of Bengal.

Farheen describes their relationship as "field of dreams where we really live everything we ever wanted." Zayed thinks the relationship "is keeping us all emotionally satisfied."

Imagine that.

the passions of aligarh

About ninety miles southeast of Delhi is a city called Aligarh. Amongst the Indian Muslims, as well as the larger South Asian Muslims, the city is as famous as Delhi itself thanks to the Aligarh Muslim University—one of the most celebrated educational institutions in the country. Many famous artists from all over the subcontinent have graduated from the school.

Perhaps this was the reason why two middle class Punjabi parents in Delhi sent their only child to the school. These parents realized early that their daughter Soniya had some artistic leanings, and they figured what better place to send her for a proper education.

"At the time, I had a hard time with their decision because Aligarh is not a big city at all," says Soniya. "But sometimes the decisions of our loved ones bring us more good things than we probably would have gotten if we decided on our own."

Aligarh proved to be one of those.

"I thought the school would be 100% Muslim, which I thought would be boring to me," remembers Soniya. "When I got there, I met people from all over the country—and from many different faiths. Suddenly, I was fascinated with the school and regretted ever thinking it would be different than what my parents had told me. I just fell in love with the student body there."

Soniya says she remembers how her parents and other family members would joke about sending her to the school where she would then meet a Hindu husband and convert to the faith. Once she got to the school, she understood why they were making that joke. For a Muslim school, there were many non-Muslim students. One of these students was a young woman named Rani, with whom Soniya became friends rather quickly.

"On the Sir Syed Day celebration, which honors the founder of the school, I met her," remembers Soniya, of her first meeting with Rani. "It was a wonderful day to meet. There was a lot of fun going on. Sweets and dancing

ıd friendships were forming. I met a lot of people that day but Rani definitely
ole the show for me. It was just an ideal first day for two girls."

After meeting, something clicked fast. "The first week I met her, we met
ıany times," recalls Soniya, laughing. "I remember we went to the lake at night
·here people wash their clothes during the day. We would just sit and talk for
ours and hours. We were inseparable!"

Within weeks, the couple felt comfortable enough with each other that
ıey both came out as lesbians to one another. Although Soniya suspected
ani was lesbian, she also thought it might have been a wishful thinking.
ani, on the other hand, was the first to take the leap. While walking in the
ıwahar Park, Rani, who is a devout Christian, reached over and held Soniya's
and. And if Soniya was unsure, she set her straight. Rani told her she was
ı love with her.

"I can't begin to explain to you how amazing that felt," shares Soniya, who
·as only nineteen at the time. "It was the most beautiful thing that I have ever
xperienced. I almost melted in my own skin. Imagine I had these thoughts
bout this woman but I was unsure about it and was torn inside. Should I tell
ɛr? Should I not? It was just perfect."

Later that day, they went back to where Rani lived and they made love. And
ıey both did not go to school the next day. And they spent the entire time
ɪlking about their shared experience.

"We put everything on the table," says Soniya. "Complete honesty. I
xpressed all that I felt for her, and explained to her that from the first day I
new she was special."

Rani, who was twenty, told Soniya that she had known about her sexuality
ıost of her life. Soniya told in return that she had realized it when she was
ine or ten. They talked about their first crushes. They talked about the shame
ɦey felt because they knew they were something, and were doing something
ɦeir parents were not expecting or would not approve of.

"There was so much we had in common," says Soniya, whose parents are
ıot devout Muslims but whose family background is pretty conservative. "We
·oth expressed everything we were afraid of. And then the question was, 'Now
·hat?' Neither of us had an answer. But it was okay because we were not
lone. We had each other, and we could do anything after that."

Their friendship grew into a lasting relationship. Rani moved in wit
Soniya near the university. And the two began to live a routine life wit
one another. Asked how they maintained a safe relationship so long in
community that is homophobic, Soniya says "everyone thought we were jus
good friends, which we were, but they just didn't know anything else wa
going on. No one knew what we were doing when we closed our door. Th
is why I love to live in India because there is a respect of privacy. Peopl
don't ask too many questions."

Rani even visited Delhi with Soniya, meeting the parents and all. No on
suspected anything. In fact, her parents told her they thought it was goo
for her to have such a close friend. "It was so perfect that they liked her. M
mother spent time with her and even allowed Rani to cook with her, whic
is something she allows on rare occasion. I loved her but it was nice that m
parents thought she was a good person," says Soniya.

The problem really came when a year later Soniya's parents wanted to marr
their daughter to a well-to-do Punjabi friend's son in Australia. Although h
promised to wait until she finishes school, the man wanted to go ahead wit
the marriage as soon as they could.

"I had no choice but to accept the arrangement," says Soniya. "Rani did nc
understand it and was very upset with me. She didn't talk to me for about
month, and was actually very hateful towards me. She moved out and began t
treat me like an enemy. I did not return any of the anger because I understoo
why she felt betrayed."

When Soniya showed that she was doing everything so they could sta
together, Rani came around. After all, this marriage was not going to take plac
in actuality until she finished school.

"I think more than anything she understood that she would probably hav
done the same," says Soniya. "Once she realized that, everything was back t
normal."

When in the same year the man ended up taking a second wife in Australi
Soniya's family had no objection when she withdrew her allegiances to hin
With her family on her side, she finally freed herself from the bonds o
marriage. Only a week after, Rani's parents came to town. This allowed Soniy
the time to meet her real "in-laws". Rani's parents fell in love with Soniya.

But whoever said good news comes in three? A week after Rani's parents left Aligarh, Rani dissolved herself from Soniya—stating that she could no longer reconcile her sexuality and her faith, and that she chose her faith. This led Soniya into a period of sadness, confusion and ultimately into a terrible depression.

She left her education and went back to Delhi, seeking refuge in her childhood home. She threw herself into helping her cousin's wedding, which she says made her life so hectic that she was able to live with her sorrow. With a bit clearer mind and somewhat healed heart, she was finally able to do something she never expected possible.

"I decided to come out to my parents," Soniya recalls. "I was not surprised when they told me they knew but I was very much taken aback when they did not condemn me. I expected them to be hateful towards me. What a good thing that was because I was preparing myself to live a life without my parents, which was not going to be any good life at all."

Soniya says she planned to join her childhood best friend in Karachi if things had not gone well with the parents. Instead, she went back to finish her school. After graduation, Soniya didn't see "any reason to stay amidst an industrial town where drama revolves around building things. While I will never forget the passionate winters that I spent there, I can't imagine living here. It is a dreadful place to me, especially emotionally."

A few years later, Soniya and Rani met at a conference in Mumbai—a city they coincidently both lived in for work. Apparently, Rani had changed her mind once more. And this time around, it was her sexuality that she chose. Not being able to reconcile the two, she left Christianity to become Atheist. And while it was now too late for their love to be rekindled, the two women have nevertheless found their way back to each other's lives—as friends. Rani is in a relationship with a French woman. Meanwhile, Soniya remains single in a city that is both bold and beautiful.

home sweet karachi

It is an early October afternoon and the streets of Karachi are warm and humid, with temperatures of mid 80s Fahrenheit. Like millions of Muslim Pakistanis, Farah has been fasting all day and is looking forward to a relaxing evening with friends. But for now, she knows she has to mingle and make her way out of the traffic in Saddar—the business center of the city, and certainly one of the busiest areas of the country.

"This is an average day in Karachi," boasts Farah, a 33-year-old lesbian from Clifton—a well-to-do neighborhood. "Only the foreigners really notice how chaotic Saddar is," she adds, continuing to say, "but we locals thrive in this atmosphere where everything seems to be falling apart and continues to go on anyway."

During Ramazan, as the Pakistanis call the Muslim holy month, Karachi as a Muslim city is often calm in the evenings. Farah is at home with her Nigerian partner and a few friends, watching an Italian movie. Her friends are diverse: two are an Australian singer and his Pakistani wife who is a television personality; another couple are gay men, both Pakistanis and in the IT industry; two straight journalists—one American, the other British; a Chinese man who is a filmmaker; and an Indian woman who teaches Yoga.

With the exception of her Nigerian girlfriend, the rest are not even Muslim. But they are all sharing an *iftar* meal—to celebrate the breaking of the fast.

"I believe in diversity," explains Farah, a freelance journalist for several newspapers across the Indian subcontinent. "I travel quite a bit. Wherever I go, I make friends. I live in a country that is half Punjabis. A country that is nearly all Muslim. Therefore, I really appreciate diversity."

The food is just as diverse as the people eating them. Among the many varieties include the South Asian fried snacks *pakoras* and *samosas*; some unripe cheese that is dipped in sugar syrup—Pakistani sweets called rasgula; New York-style pizza and cheesecakes; a Nigerian thick paste of maize called

fu; and lots of Chinese fortune cookies. Mango, guava, lemon juices are all available, as well as Coca-Cola products.

Later, after the movie is over and everyone had eaten, the topic of the conversation turns to Ramadan and fasting.

"I just wish I could be like you," says Andy, the Chinese journalist. "You make a big sacrifice by not eating. I heard from some colleagues that Islam does not accept gays and lesbians. It must be tough being a lesbian and Muslim, though?"

"I keep telling her it is pointless to fast," interjects Maimuna, Farah's girlfriend. "What is the point? Why do you fast when you are lesbian and everyone is telling you hell waits? Why do you do this to yourself?" Maimuna asks as she turns to Farah.

Farah sits up, puts a pillow on her lap and says, "When I was a little girl, fasting was all I really wanted to do," she explains. "When I grew up, and realized I was a lesbian and will probably go to hell for this, I still wanted to fast. I love how I feel when I fast, but sure I have my struggles. It is supposed to be holy, and I must believe it is for all."

"But that is not at all how it is!" Maimuna argues, continuing to say, "I was taught that Ramadan frees people. It does not free me. I remember all the bad things people said to me when I came out. My own very uncle said I should die a painful death."

Farah grew up in a nonreligious environment. Arts were especially appreciated in the family, with both parents being part of the community—father being a painter and the mother a poet. However, there was a sense of pride in one's Muslim identity and deep feelings of dishonor when one breaks way with tradition, says Farah.

"My mother read old Urdu poetry to us," Farah tells her friends. "These poets showed their pride with their faith and culture in most unsubtle couplets. We listened to *qawali* [devotional music] many nights while we danced with each other. Yet everyone in my family still rejected me," she adds with a sad tone. "It is as if I betrayed them someway. Of course, I have my struggles with Islam. But I feel a sense of home when I fast or do *namaz* [prayers]."

Later, after everyone had left, Farah looks back on her journey.

"My friends probably see me as a weak person," she says, "but they don't know what I have gone through. It is very hard to grow up in a country with an ideology and culture that is completely different from who you are. I always felt like I was an outsider."

Eleven years earlier, she left home for London. She told her family that she was going there to study Journalism. But in reality, Farah was running away from home. Once in England, she began living her life as lesbian—a life she now says is possible here in Pakistan.

"For the first time in my life, I was able to feel I belonged," she says of dancing at parties full of women in London. "I vowed to never leave. It was really great meeting people from every corner of the world."

After many sexual experiences, she settled with a French doctor—much older, and was far more settled into the English culture than Farah. The two were very much attracted to their differences, says Farah, who admits liking the way it felt to be with an older woman.

"She didn't treat me like a child," says Farah, "but there was definitely some mothering going on. I think I felt safe with her the same way I did with my own mother."

Now that she was in a loving relationship, she felt strong enough that she could came out to her family. She imagined that it would be hard for her family however she never expected to be treated the way she was.

"My father told me that I was no longer his daughter," says Farah, "and mother was not any better. She just refused to talk to me."

For nearly a year, this was the case. When her sister was getting married Farah came for the wedding. And, somehow, the family began to see she was still the same person.

"My mother said 'I expected you to look like someone else,'" recalls Farah "and my sister, whom I had talked to on the phone for nearly every week since I was gone, said she thought I was pretending to be the same person."

When the relationship with her girlfriend went soar, Farah headed home.

"I had no idea what it was like to feel as though you don't belong until I went to a foreign country," she says, showing pictures from her life in England "I was in a country where most people don't celebrate Muslim holidays, where *Eid* went by as though just another day and the holy month came and went without much notice. I enjoyed that for the first few years, but I could not exist there. Of course, there are neighborhoods in England with a number of Muslims. But it is still the same, somehow."

Though her relationship with her family is not quiet as it was, today there is an understanding that she is entitled to her own life. Her family no longer tries to set her up with presumed perfect matches, and though she still gets those "odd looks" at family functions from relatives, she is still part of the family.

"Everything is okay," she says, with a smile, "I'm okay."

delicious memories in xinjiang

There are forty million Muslims and forty thousand mosques in China. alf of those mosques are in the Xinjiang region alone. Set at the foot of the orious Tianshan Mountains and just south of the Junggar Basin, the capital f the region, Urumqi, booms with cultural diversity and natural wonderment imatched anywhere else in the entire country. In this great city, there is a ruggle between the modern and the traditional.

Urumqi is a metropolis. For every one-foot square, there are a hundred and n people. It has a well developed downtown, with a beautiful skyline and iptivating designs of neighborhoods. If you walk around town, you will agree iat most people are modern—the way they are dressed, the way they carry iemselves and the way they are in general. Yet, this city is very traditional.

And Ma, a young woman in her early thirties, was born right into this intradiction. At the tender young age of ten, Ma decided she wanted to be a cholar when she grew up.

"Sitting at my house, reading the Qur'an," she says, "I felt a call to becoming irsed in the faith. It was something inside of me I cannot explain."

Although there is a great tradition of Islam in China, which allows women iore participation in the faith than perhaps anywhere else in the Muslim World, iere still was much struggle in her own family. When Ma turned sixteen, her father ild her he would be marrying her soon to some man he was friends with.

"Without asking me how I would feel," Ma remembers, "my father just ild me I would become the wife of so and so. This was perhaps okay in my ilture but I did not like it. And I made it clear to my father that I did not like at all."

In Han tradition, when it comes to marriage a woman follows the desires f her family over her own. But Ma had too many desires.

"Ever since I was maybe ten," she says, as she giggles, "I was in love with woman in our neighborhood. She was a doctor. This is not that unusual but

or me it was exotic. She was the only woman doctor in my area that I knew.
very morning, as she would leave for work, I would sit and fantasize being
timate with her. I was only ten!"

After many years of fantasy, Ma deeply believed she was in love with the
oman and knew marriage would disrupt that feeling.

"When you are married, you have no time to think about yourself," she says,
ith a serious tone, "you have in-laws and other family to think of; you have a
usband whom you need to be available to his needs; and are otherwise busy
ith everything married life demands."

Not sure what to do, Ma consulted with one of her mentors—a teacher from
:hool. The teacher, who happened to be a female, told her to agree to marriage.

"She said I had no choice," remembers Ma. "She told me to forget about
ıy infatuation with the woman and just get married. So I agreed to the
ıarriage."

Married life was not as bad at all as she thought. Her husband was very kind
) her, and he spent most of the day away from the house and working. And
ecause he was making good income, he was able to afford a maid for his wife
hen she got pregnant with their first child. And this created a different bliss
ı her new life.

"She was of Kazakh background," says Ma, who belongs to the largest
:oup in the area—the Han. "Her name was Adila. She was a very beautiful
ırl with a very sweet smile. I fell in love with her immediately and completely.
his was weird because I also fell in love with my husband."

Although she loved her husband, Ma says she loved him for being so kind
) her and giving her a life of happiness. Almost immediately after marriage,
Ia had gotten pregnant and gave birth to a daughter.

But with Adila, Ma found passion. The two women felt like they were soul
ıates. They spent most of their time with each other. During the day, while
er husband was away, Ma and Adila studied Islam together. Both of them
rere very spiritual, and they sought acceptance from the faith.

"We found passages in the Qur'an that we believed accepted our feelings for
ach other," she says. "It talked about how God created us all from one soul and
ow from that soul came many others. So we didn't think God needed us to
rocreate or to just be with men only because now we have billions of souls."

But time with Adila was not just restricted to the day hours. At night whe her husband was home, Ma would spend more time with her lover while he husband read books and meditated. She always made sure she made love wit Adila first, only after then would she shower and make love with her husban And while she did not make love with her husband every night, she made lov with Adila sometimes two and three times a day.

"Everything in my life was perfect," she says of the time. "I was the happies You know, I'm very modest person but I want to say that I never had orgas until I made love with Adila."

After several years of good life, something horrible happened. One da after she was going home from a local supermarket, a city bus ran over Adil She was killed immediately. Adila was only nineteen. And twenty-one year ol Ma was devastated.

Because she was from a very poor family, Adila was not planning to ge married but continue to work in the city to make income for her family back i the villages. In truth, it was because she was in love with Ma and didn't want t be away from her. And although she could still work and be married, like man women do in the area, she chose to spend most of her time with Ma.

Now, it has been seven years. Ma is still mourning the loss. Not a day goe by, she says, that she doesn't remember her Adila. Ma says if she were alive, th two would still have been together. Her husband suspects the two were mor than friends but he never questioned Ma about it. And Ma thinks he accep it.

persian love in istanbul

Bahar is going through many small stores in the spice market of Istanbul, known to locals as *Misir Carsisi* (Egyptian Bazaar). It is Thursday afternoon and she is shopping for all sorts of spices needed to make a grand Persian meal for her partner's fortieth birthday dinner that night.

"She loves *ghormeh sabzi* [a stew served with basmati rice]," says the 42-year-old Bahar of her partner. "I would love to make it for her, but unlike many Persians she prefers it made with fish. Don't ask me why. It is a strange thing. Fortunately, we all like it anyway when she makes it. She is an amazing cook. Tonight she is not allowed to touch a thing. She is to sit back and enjoy like the Queen she is."

Bahar owns a jewelry store in the Grand Bazaar, known to the locals as *Kapalicarsi*. In 1992 she fled Tehran, where she was born and raised, because of increased harassment to queer women in the city. Since she sold her jewelry store in one of Tehran's most popular malls, she had some money when she arrived in Istanbul. Money does not buy everything, however, found out Bahar.

"I didn't know what to do," remembers Bahar, who moved to Istanbul for its large Persian community. "I didn't know anyone. My family was in Iran, and I had no friends in Turkey. The man who smuggled me out of Iran dropped me in a horrible hotel. He didn't introduce me to anyone, and I didn't speak Turkish. It was a very difficult time."

Bahar's family is Jewish, and that added to the pressure being new in a country that is nearly all Muslim. Although Turkey has a number of Jews close to that of Iran, says Bahar, they are just not as visible.

"We complained in Iran," says Bahar, laughing, "but in Iran there are famous Jews. You have Jewish MP. There is a famous Jewish hospital in Tehran. And you know about Iranian Jews in the world who are famous like the Israeli president or American actors. But in Turkey, nothing."

One day as she was walking about, she met a woman named Manizha, who turned out to be a Persian from Afghanistan. "She was so happy to meet me," says Manizha, who was born and raised in Kabul. "We are called Tajik. Our language, our culture, as well as our ancestry, are all Persian."

The women spoke in Persian, and they say they both knew right away they were lesbians. "There was just something about the way she looked at me," says Bahar, "almost with Persian *aashegh* [love]. I was delighted because not only did I find a Persian sister but I found a lesbian to boost!"

It was the beginning of a love affair.

Manizha is from a Muslim family, and says she never met a Persian Jew before Bahar.

"I didn't know right away," says Manizha, who is not religious. "It just made me step back a little, I think, because it was as if there was a little betrayal—although I fully know Judaism is not any less Persian than Islam is, for both are foreign faiths imported to us."

Bahar, on the other hand, had more troubles with Manizha's other life. At the time, Manizha had gotten a divorce from her husband a few weeks earlier (via telephone, strangely enough) and was the sole caretaker of their four children. The husband had left for Toronto about a year before the two women had met.

"I just wasn't sure if I was really ready for that kind of responsibility," says Bahar. "I was completely in love with Manizha—but to be a mother? That was not in my plan. I considered myself a butch lesbian. I never envisioned of having children. When I was younger, my family tried many times to have me married. It never worked. I wanted to live the rest of my life with the pleasures and no worries. But we don't really plan our lives as well as we think we have."

While Bahar had many years to get used to being the boss of her life, Manizha was different. It was the first year of her life without a "guardian." She, her husband, and their children moved from Kabul in 1988 in an effort to find a better life. And since then she had been guided by him everywhere. When he left for Canada, she was suddenly dropped into a role she was not comfortable with.

"I was not used to making all the decisions in my family," remembers Manizha. "I had become very depressed, and begun to hate my life. Eventually,

ay husband got very tired of my complete negative outlook on a relationship
nd he asked for a divorce."

After some months of struggle, the women decided to be together. Manizha
ad learned to accept Bahar's faith into her perception of the Persian culture,
nd Bahar had gained some insights to lesbian parenting from her partner.

"Now it is natural," jokes Bahar. "I yell as good as her! Seriously, I have found
to be true that we adapt to our lives. I love these children today as if they were
ut from my own body. I can't imagine my life without them. Manizha tells me
ll the time that I'm a better mother than she is. I don't know about that one but
think I have a lot of what it takes to be a mother. We both do."

As part of the grand Persian dinner, Bahar will be preparing *shirini tar*—
terally "wet deserts" because they are custard and crème filled pastries, cakes
nd special ice creams. For the children, says Bahar, everything else is to be
verlooked.

After dinner, Bahar plans to leave the kids with the oldest son (he is in
is late teens) and take her partner to a movie, a disco and then spend the
ight at a local château where she plans to "make love to the woman until she
ppreciates the forties!"

istanbul's street girls

In the Middle East, there is often only one country where queer Muslims an safely escape to. That is Turkey. The other country, of course, is Israel, ut a lot of these Muslims in the Middle East, and in the world at large, have rejudices against Israel. But Turkey is a respected "Muslim" country. The ountry has a rich tradition of being tolerant to queer people. But even in aradise, there is bound to be some problems.

"I can live here but I also encounter a lot of problems," says Loula, a male->-female pre-op transsexual who lives in Istanbul.

Turkey has been problematic for transsexuals today and in the past. While all ueer people face discrimination, Turkish transsexuals face extra discriminations ased on the fact that most of them really "cannot" be in the closet because nany dress against their "biological" genders, take hormones to shift the state f their looks, and even undergo gender reassignment surgeries—all part of n obviousness they cannot get away from.

"I still face discrimination," says Demet, a political activist who happens ɔ be a male-to-female transsexual who has gone under the knife and is now ompletely a woman. "For many of these [heterosexual] people, it does not hange the fact. I still represent something they do not want to acknowledge. cannot tell you how many times I have been insulted and threatened, even fter the surgery."

And Demet enjoys something most transsexuals don't have—she is petite, mall and frail looking woman. If she didn't speak, at which point you would ear a bit deep voice, you would never know she was "born" a man. This is ιot the case with many.

"I ran away from Iran to be come here," says Loula, who at six-feet-two-ιches stands to be a tall woman, aside from the fact that she is "too" muscular ɔr a female in the Turkish culture and that she has a very deep voice. "Sure, 'm not scared to get killed here but I face the same discrimination as I did in

hran. People look at me, and they hear my voice, and it does not add up for
em. So instead of asking me nicely what is the matter, they turn to abuse.
is is their only way of dealing with someone like myself."

And on streets like Taksim—a notorious street for transsexual prostitutes
d those who indulge in their services—danger is everywhere.

"I get beaten all the time," says Loula, "it is normal on this street. But I have
be here or I will be nowhere. If I must die, at least I want to die trying to
ake a living."

Leaders like Demet say these transsexual prostitutes have no other way.
hen Loula came to Istanbul a few years ago, she knew no one. Like many
nssexuals who immigrate into Turkey, Loula ended up on the streets—selling
r body to anyone who would consider it.

"I had no choice," she recalls. "I did not speak the Turkish language, and
lid not have any friends or family to help me. I met an Iranian lesbian who
troduced me to an Iranian transsexual who was a prostitute. She told me to
in her. I didn't start to make a lot of money very fast."

Prostitution is plentiful in Turkey, especially Istanbul area where there
e an estimated ten thousand prostitutes, most of whom can be found in
e Beyoglu district. Brothels and red-light districts are common throughout
ge cities in Turkey. A lot of these prostitutes are transsexuals, most of
em born outside of Turkey.

"If you are transsexual but not Turkish," says Ishtar, a Turkish male-to-
male pre-op who lightens her skin, wears blue contact lenses and has dyed
r hair blonde, "you enjoy a certain freedom. Somehow, people here don't
ink you are as bad as someone like me who happens to be from Turkey. For
is reason, many of us Turkish transsexuals go to great lengths to pretend we
e not Turkish. Sometimes it can save your life!"

Most transsexual prostitutes turn to the business because they are not
owed to work in many places, say experts like Demet. And the more they
e faced with these pressures, the more they turn to prostitution even if their
es are endangered.

"They have no other chance," says Meltem Firatli, a journalist who works for
aftalik, a popular news magazine. "In fact, because of the pressure on them,
ey are aggressive. It is the only way they can make their living," she adds.

For Samira, a beautiful young transsexual, it is a life forced by the public

"I am who I am," she says. "This is the only job I can have to support i life. I have tried to find other sources of work but I have been turned dov many times. Even when I was hired elsewhere, the men expected sexual favo At least on the streets I can decide how much I want to make."

Samira is Egyptian. Seven years ago, her family disowned her and threw h out of the house at the young age of fourteen. Her family decided to send th boy to a highly conservative Muslim school, forcing Samira to come out.

"A woman friend of mine gave me some gold, which I sold and used come here," she says. "I only had with me less than $25. Turkey was expensi and there were no jobs anywhere."

Another transsexual prostitute, who goes by the name Lillie, says that son Middle Eastern countries pressure gay men to also become women.

"A gay man is not allowed to be man in many parts of the Arab worlc says Lillie, one of the handful who has had the surgery. "The only way is to feminine, and we do that. And then we can't work so we become prostitut What other choices have we?"

A gay man, Yilditz, who was born and raised in Istanbul, agrees wi Lillie.

"It is hard because they don't understand," he says. "They say if you li other men then join women. Only women can like men. I was very feminir I thought it would be easier."

Today, although he has gone back to being a "man," Yilditz still identifi with the community. Some nights he will dress up as a woman and go wi some of his old friends for a night of sexual favors.

"I do have a regular job at a bank," he confesses,."It is just that I rememb how liberating it felt sometimes. Not all the prostitutes on the streets a unhappy with their lives."

Turkey's complicated relationship with its transsexuals can be seen throu Bulent Ersoy, a transsexual who is perhaps the most popular Turkish singer tod:

"People hate her but they also love her," says Loula. "This is who we a in Turkey. Everyday, you don't know whether you will get smiles or will beaten. The police and the civilians are the same. No one knows what happe from one day to the next."

Since the Islamic political parties have gotten more popular in Istanbul in recent years, however, the crackdown on the transsexual community has been a growing problem. More and more brothels close down after police harassments, after the deaths of transsexuals pushed onto the highways by the police, and the transsexuals are now more careful.

"A lot of these political groups feel that if they are more aggressive against groups deemed to be living in sin, they will get larger support of the conservative voters," reasons Firatli. "The only way to protect the disadvantaged groups is to pressure the government. The European Union is a good source of pressure. Also, the United Nations can be involved."

In the meantime, women like Loula have to make a living. And their jobs can be just as dangerous as their gender identity. One night, Loula met a young man who was really attracted to her but who later felt embarrassed when he realized she had a penis.

"He freaked out and beat me very hard," she says. "I lost one tooth, and he severed my nose. I quit working for months after that, fearing something like that might happen to me again."

But sooner or later, abused transsexuals find their way back to the streets. Samira also returned to the streets once after being hospitalized for weeks due to a gang attack. They broke her arm, two ribs and four of her front teeth.

"As soon as I healed, I had to go back to pay back those who lent me some money for the medical expenses," Samira recalls. "I was very afraid but I knew there was no other way to make money. I had to take drugs to force myself."

Both Loula and Samira agree that the advantages of the streets outweigh the disadvantages. Because of the kind of money she makes, Samira was able to pay for gender reassignment surgery. But she says her greatest achievement is her home, which she bought after many years of saving.

"It is just great to come home and know it is mine," she says.

For Loula, buying a home is not even on the radar. Right now, her priorities lie in making enough just to be able to afford a place to rent and food.

"I really don't have big ambitions," she says. "I just want to survive. I sell myself enough so that I am not homeless or hungry. That is all I can do now."

In a country like Turkey, she can always change her mind later.

summers in foros

On the southern tip of the Crimean Peninsula, between Sevastopol and
alta, there is a resort town called Foros. It is one of the many towns and
llages situated on the Black Sea that are part of the Russian Riviera.

In Foros, summer is the season to shine. Folks flock all over the
gion to see and to be seen. From Simferopol, the capital, to Yalta, the
ngest trolleybus route in the world delivers people to their most-desired
estinations.

One such summer brought a Muslim woman named Mina.

"I just fell in love with it, and I decided to stay," says the 44-year-old Turkish-
orn Mina. "My parents loved this land. Somehow I feel like it was destined
or me to come back here, even though they are no longer living. It is as if God
compensating for them for their loss through me."

She is one of the thousands of Crimean Tatars who returned after Ukraine's
ndependence from the Soviet Union. Her parents were many of the Tatars
xiled from their homeland by Joseph Stalin's Soviet government.

"As a child, I lived through the horrific stories my parents told about their
eparture from Qirim [Crimea]," remembers Mina. "They settled in Turkey.
'hat is where my sister and I were born. It is very strange that, even though I
as born in Turkey, I feel like Crimea is my homeland. I feel very sad that they
re not here to share it with me. It would have been so satisfying to them to
ve and work in their country of birth."

Although she was born and raised in Turkey, Mina says she always felt an
utside in her country.

"The way people would react to me always made me aware of my original
oots," she says, "somehow, I always felt like I had to defend myself. I mean, it
 funny because I was born in Izzir—a big city. Yet, this was happening to me.
'he truth is that I never felt I belonged in Turkey because the Turkish people
lt I was not Turkish. It is quite sad, actually."

In the late 1990s, after she visited the town by the sea, Mina sold her partment in Istanbul and moved to Foros. She bought a house near the beach, nd now hosts lesbian events wither her partner four times a year for women :om Russia (where her partner is from) and Turkey.

"Most of the year, we spend it in Simferopol, which is a very active and razy metropolis," says Mina, "so we love coming down here for the summer nd partying a few times a year. It is a holiday and a good cause all rolled into ne. Can I ask for more?"

Ekaterina, Mina's partner, has a 21-year-old son from a previous heterosexual narriage, one that lasted less than a year. The couple is also raising Ekaterina's vo nieces. Since they all live together, the kids refer to Mina as mother to ʻhich she considers an honor.

"It makes me feel good, which is a surprise to me," she says, laughing, "I ıst never wanted to have children. I thought it was stupid to have children. ʃut now, things are different. I love our children. They make our lives more ıteresting, I think. It is such an honor when they look up to me."

And on top of parenting, the couple run a restaurant together. Mina says, ·ecause of their busy lives, she has less to worry about what others think about .er sexuality.

"My sister is very opposed to my lifestyle," says Mina, who has been out ɔ her sister since she realized she was a lesbian in her late teens. "She always ·elieved I would get married someday and be a wife. When she figured out that ʻas not going to happen, she began to deal with her feelings about lesbianism. Jnfortunately, they were not good feelings. It took many years of healing and truggle before she could accept it. And now we have a bigger obstacle."

Her sister is married to a very conservative politician in Turkey, says Mina.)ver the years, the husband has made her sister more and more conservative. \s would be expected, he bars the sister from communicating much or visiting ʻith Mina. Because of this they have not seen each other for over three years. \nd Mina longs to see her sister.

"Not being allowed to see my nieces and nephews hurts more than nything," says Mina. "I have accepted that not everyone is going to be alright ʻith who I'm. It is okay. I wish someday I can visit my sister and her children ʻhenever I want—without fearing her husband is going to beat her, humiliate

her, or do any of the things he does. It is a long shot but I have to believe i
She is all I hav, as far as my biological family goes."

Mina feels betrayed by her sister.

"When our mother passed away, we made a promise to be in each other'
lives above all others. She broke that promise, but I understand. It is he
husband."

It hadn't always been as easy to be so self-loving. Mina remembers time
as a child where she would lock herself in the bathroom and cry because sh
knew she couldn't change her sexuality.

"Being a tomboy in a Muslim country is not something that you can get awa
with without suffering serious consequences," Mina says of her childhood. "
was denied friendships by parents who didn't think I was girly enough for thei
daughters. I remember feeling sick every time my mother would be ashame
of my uncontrollable behavior of masculinity. I used to pray God over an
over to fix me somehow. What can you do, you know?"

When she moved to the big city of Istabul at the age of thirty, Mina fel
a sense of relief. There she was in a new city, not knowing many people an
being able to live her life the way she wanted to live—without fearing sh
would be badmouthed by people she knew.

"Once I was invited to a lesbian party in Beyoglu [a district in Istanbul],
remembers Mina. "I see myself even now getting big goose bumps. It was
defining and life-altering moment in my life to have seen so many women lik
myself gathered in one place. After that, everything was okay."

sacrifices in sarajevo

In Sarajevo, there is a charming district called Stari Grad. It is perhaps the most beautiful area of the city, and certainly the oldest. The name actually means "old town" and its heart is the *Baščaršija*, the Turkish old market that is the birthplace of the city.

The district's architecture combines those influences of the Ottoman and Europe. For example, in the same area, you have the Gazi Husrev-Beg Mosque, built during the 1500s; the Sarajevo Cathedral, built in the 1800s; and the Ashkenazi Synagogue, built in the early 1900s. They all showcase some sort of a melting pot of the East and West.

And like its history, Stari Grad is known to be the bohemian district where misfits are welcomed. When Mirza was growing up, he remembers a booming neighborhood full of artists, poets and dancers—where they drank wine while the imams passed by without condemnation. It was a common knowledge within the community for some of these artists to have led alternative sexual lives, too.

"I used to peak through the doors of mixed parties in the neighborhood and I recall seeing men dancing together, kissing on the lips while they fondled each other," says Mirza, a 37-year-old gay man born and raised in the district. "Everything was tolerated. All of Sarajevo used to be like that for me. Gay and straight people mixed freely without bad feelings between them."

Mirza's father owned a little shop in the Baščaršija, and he remembers seeing all sorts of clientele come through the door. One of the customers stands out in his mind.

"It was during a World Cup season and my father was selling something I don't recall right now to a beautiful woman. She was dressed in tight soccer outfit, and I remember thinking that her hair was so bright and seeing how big her breasts were. But under all that make up and giggle, she had a man's voice.

was a transsexual! I am still amazed that my father didn't say a word about
This is tolerance."

When he was a teenager, Mirza, who is from a Muslim family, met and fell
love with an older Christian man named Stefan. Stefan was from Mostar,
own south of Sarajevo. Although Muslim, Mirza's family didn't mind that
eir son was "close friends" with a Christian or a Serb.

"Stefan was a winemaker who came to Sarajevo on a regular basis,"
members Mirza. "He loved to come to Stari Grad because people here didn't
re about anything. He would offer wine to both heterosexual and homosexual
uslims, and they would take it! There were many people like that who were
pable of so much tolerance."

According to Mirza, those days are over now.

"Now things are different," he says. "The tolerance is gone. Gay people
ck with each other. We don't mix with the straight community. There is some
spoken fear between all of us."

Mirza says when the war broke out in the early 1990s it was no longer safe
r the queer folk to trust others because of continued violence against the
mmunity. The queers began to help each other and sticked with each other
ore and more. This led to them becoming a sort of "separate" community
thin a community. And apparently these new habits are hard to change.

"I now exclusively go to gay parties," says Mirza, who happens to be
writer hoping to publish some of his novels about his happy childhood
Stari Grad. "I don't really have many straight friends. Usually they are
ople I met through work. Things have really changed here. Slowly we let
all of our straight friends. It is a sad realization about our situation in the
ciety today. This whole country was completely affected and changed by
at war."

Although Mirza works for a newspaper headquartered in Novi Grad, another
strict far from Stari Grad, he refuses to give up his old town apartment and
ys commuting is worth it. Most of the gays are slowly moving out of the
strict, he says, including his long-term ex-boyfriend who now lives in another
d newer district called Novo Sarajevo.

"When Emir moved out from here, I have to say that I too was tempted
leave," says Mirza. "But then it occurred to me that Stari Grad is my home.

I don't care if all of my friends move away, I have to be here. I tried to l elsewhere, but it doesn't work for me."

Mirza and Emir had been together for years. The two met when Emi mother, who had met Mirza when she worked with his family as an interi designer, invited them for dinner to her house and introduced them. Becau their interests are completely different, they have run into some obstacles ov the years. But none like Emir's move to Novo Sarajevo.

"It was a difficult time for both of us," remembers Mirza. "Emir has bee working with the company he works for since 1995, and when his compai relocated he had to follow them because he never liked commuting. I know l still blames me for not moving as well."

Mirza tried to make it work with Emir for months after the move, but the relationship continued to deteriorate because they were no longer able to s each other on a daily basis. Mirza didn't want to go to Novo Sarajevo a lot ai Emir didn't want to come to Stari Grad as much. They began to fight mo and more until they both realized it was easier and safer for them to separa than stay on course.

But Mirza defends his insisting on living in Stari Grad.

"There is not another part of the world that makes feel the way I feel wh(I am here. I was born here, I want to live here, and hopefully I will be allow(to spend my final moments here."

Although gays might prefer the newer areas of the city, Mirza says that tl tourists are still fascinated by the old eastern charm of Stari Grad. And whi he had sacrificed so much to be living here, he couldn't be happier.

GLOSSARY

ashegh	word for love in many Muslim nations
shna	boy who is sexually active with older men in Afghanistan
yatollah	word for Sign of God; term for scholars in Shi'ism
edegh	passive male in Afghanistan
helo kebob	popular Iranian grilled meat, served with basmati rice
Eid	word for festival; a Muslim holiday
atwa	word for decree; opinion issued by an Islamic scholar
fu	Nigerian dish made out of maize
ur	Sudanese people from the region Darfur
abadh	word for girl in Somali, especially in the North
hormeh sabzi	Iranian stew, served with basmati rice
Iausa	Nigerian people, and mostly Muslim
Iar	meal to break the fasting with during Ramadan
mam	Islamic leader; often leader of a moque
anjaweed	armed militia in Sudan, especially in the Darfur region
nn	demons in Islam
ajawas	camel panniers in Persian cultures
itenge	kind of African clothing
uch-i-safari	feminine men used for sexual pleasure in Afghanistan
utchi	ethnic group in Kenya from South Asian background
garoone	insulting word for gay men in Somalia
adrassa	Muslim school
Iajles	Iranian legislative body with about 300 members
anyak	insulting term for gay men in some Arab countries
Iassaleit	Sudanese tribe
ehboob	male lover

muhathara	Muslim sermon, which relates to current events
namaz	word for ritual prayer in Turkish, Urdu, and Persian
Nellywood	Nigerian film industry
pakora	South Asian deep-fried snack
qawali	form of Sufi devotional music, popular in Pakistan
Ramadan	ninth month in the Muslim calender, with an all-month fasting
rasgula	Pakistani dessert with unripe cheese dipped in sugar syrup
samosa	deep fried snack popular across the Muslim World
sheesha	Arabic word for hookah; water pipe for smoking
sheikh	Islamic scholar
Shi'ism	Islamic denomination
Shaitan	Islamic word for Devil
Sharia	Islamic law
souk	Arabic word for market
shirini tar	Persian custard filled pastries, cakes, and special ice cream
Sufism	a mystical Muslim path
Sunnism	an Islamic denomination
surma	dark toxic eyeliner
wadi	Arabic word for riverbed
wasagaji	word for lesbians in Swahili
Waqooyi	region in northern Somalia
wasagaji	word for lesbians in Swahili
Xinjiang	predominantly Muslim region in China
Yoruba	Nigerian people, mostly non-Muslim
Zaghawa	Sudanese tribe
Zayuna	gay neighborhood in Baghdad

LIST OF IMAGES

Printed in the United Kingdom
by Lightning Source UK Ltd.
132227UK00001B/351/P